LEADERSHIP AND MANAGEMENT DEVELOPMENT IN EDUCATION

'Educational Leadership for Social Justice' Series
Series Editor: David Middlewood

Tony Bush and David Middlewood *Leading and Managing People in Education* 2005
Jacky Lumby with Marianne Coleman *Leadership and Diversity* 2007
David Middlewood and Richard Parker *Leading and Managing Extended Schools* 2009

Leadership and Management Development in Education

Tony Bush

SSAGE

Los Angeles • London • New Delhi • Singapore

First published 2008

SAGE Publications Ltd
1 Oliver's Yard
55 City Road
London EC1Y 1SP

SAGE Publications Inc.
2455 Teller Road
Thousand Oaks, California 91320

SAGE Publications India Pvt Ltd
B 1/I 1 Mohan Cooperative Industrial Area
Mathura Road
New Delhi 110 044

SAGE Publications Asia-Pacific Pte Ltd
33 Pekin Street #02-01
Far East Square
Singapore 048763

Library of Congress Control Number: 2007940390

British Library Cataloguing in Publication data

A catalogue record for this book is available from the British Library

ISBN 978-1-4129-2180-0
ISBN 978-1-4129-2181-7 (pbk)

Typeset by Dorwyn, Wells, Somerset
Printed in Great Britain by T.J. International, Padstow, Cornwall
Printed on paper from sustainable resources

Contents

Notes on the author

Tony Bush is Professor of Educational Leadership at the University of Warwick and previously held similar posts at the universities of Leicester, Reading and Lincoln. He has experience as a teacher and middle manager in secondary schools and as a professional officer with a local authority. He has wide international experience, having been a visiting professor, external examiner, consultant or invited keynote speaker in Australia, China, Germany, Greece, Hong Kong, New Zealand, Norway, Portugal, the Seychelles, Singapore and South Africa. He has published extensively, including his best-selling trilogy of books on Theories of Educational Leadership and Management. He has directed many research and evaluation projects on aspects of leadership and leadership development, notably for the English National College for School Leadership, and in South Africa. He is also the editor of the leading international journal, *Educational Management, Administration and Leadership*.

Series Editor's Foreword

This series of books recognises that leadership in education in the twenty-first century has an increasingly important role in the transformation of society. Leaders have an onerous responsibility to address issues which affect the development of greater social justice in their nations' attempts to ensure their economic futures.

For those in education, leadership now involves confronting issues such as those of equity, inclusion and diversity, in stimulating the changes needed for the embedding of social justice. Such changes can only be effected by people, which is why the first book in the series focused on leading and managing people (Bush and Middlewood 2005). However, without an adequate supply of effective leaders, these changes simply will not happen. To be effective, they need to be well prepared, trained and developed. This book deals with the topic of how educational leaders are, and perhaps might be, prepared and developed for their crucial roles.

No author can be better qualified to write such a book than Tony Bush, one of the leading researchers and writers on educational leadership, especially in the international context, and this authoritative text is the result of many years of personal research in many countries. This long-needed book gives a comprehensive overview of international practice in this field, covering both developed and developing nations. Practice is shown to vary widely, according to context, culture and, inevitably, available resources. Despite the variety of practice, Tony Bush is able to draw out the commonalities as well as the differences, showing, for example, how the content of leadership preparation programmes can be similar despite the diversity of contexts.

The author also analyses the trends in leadership preparation and development which are discernible across differing contexts, for example, the shift in emphasis from content to process and, tellingly, the need to help leaders prepare to address major issues such as diversity and inclusion in increasingly pluralistic societies.

There are no simple answers to the question 'What is the best way to prepare and develop leaders in education?' However, this masterly book not only gives the fullest possible picture and expert analysis of the field, but it will stimulate debate among professional practitioners and academics alike, and prove an invaluable resource for those seeking these answers.

David Middlewood

Preface

The significance of effective leadership and management for the successful operation of schools and colleges is widely acknowledged in the twenty-first century. There is growing recognition that the quality of leaders, and leadership, is critical if schools are to produce the best possible outcomes for their learners, and their stakeholders. The longstanding appreciation of the vital role of teachers is belatedly being matched by an understanding that skilled leadership is also required if schools and colleges are to thrive.

The traditional view in many countries is that school principals and senior staff need only to be qualified and experienced teachers. However, there is now an emerging recognition that leadership is a parallel, if not separate, profession and requires specific preparation. This has led many countries to introduce formal development opportunities for aspiring and practising principals. In countries as diverse as Canada, England, France, Scotland and the USA, a formal leadership qualification is required *before* senior leaders take up their posts. Elsewhere, there is more reliance on in-service opportunities. The nature of the development process varies in line with the specific context, but the overall trend is towards preparing and developing leaders as a key dimension of school improvement.

The landscape of leadership development in England has been transformed by the opening, and subsequent expansion, of the National College for School Leadership (NCSL). The College provides a raft of programmes for middle leaders, deputy heads, aspiring heads, new heads, experienced leaders and teams. This ambitious provision is supported by an active research function. The NCSL has had a major impact on school leadership in England and has also influenced change in many other countries.

This book examines the reasons for the expansion of leadership preparation and training, and assesses the various modes of development in use in many countries. It is underpinned by the view that leaders should have an entitlement to appropriate preparation and support for their important and onerous role in leading educational change. To appoint school principals without specific preparation is a gamble, and we should not gamble with children's education.

Chapter 1 sets the scene by discussing the reasons for the enhanced global interest in the role of school leaders. It assesses the differences between leadership and management, and argues that both are essential if schools and colleges are to thrive. It also examines the evidence that effective leadership is critical to school improvement.

While the importance of leadership and management is increasingly recognised, much less is known about which leadership behaviours are most likely to promote successful schooling. Chapter 2 examines the various models of leadership and assesses the evidence of their effectiveness. There is great interest in 'instructional leadership' because of the widespread view that the main function of schools is to promote student learning. Transformational leadership is widely advocated because of its potential to harness stakeholder support for the school's (or leader's) vision but there is some concern that this may be a vehicle for imposing leaders', or governments', priorities on teachers, pupils and communities. These and other models are subject to scrutiny in this chapter.

Chapter 3 addresses the significance of leadership and management development in education. It points to the emergence of four imperatives; the expanded role of school leaders, the increasing complexity of school contexts, the moral case for leadership preparation, and the growing evidence that effective development makes a difference.

Chapter 4 discusses the curriculum for leadership development. There is great diversity in the content of preparation and training programmes but there is an emerging 'core' around the need to provide for the management of teaching and learning, an awareness of the legal and policy framework for leadership, the need for effective management of people and resources, and a recognition that efficient administration is required to keep schools 'on track'. In the twenty-first century, there has been increasing interest in the 'delivery' of programmes and on the processes by which leadership learning is enhanced. Networking, mentoring, coaching and facilitation are among the strategies used in several countries and there is growing evidence of their effectiveness.

Chapter 5 focuses on preparation and support for leaders in developed countries. These are mostly rich nations and decisions about the shape and scope of leadership preparation are based on perceptions of need and appropriateness rather than being circumscribed by limited funding. The chapter examines five stages of development: leadership succession, preparation, selection, induction and ongoing in-service development.

As we noted earlier, the NCSL is a powerful symbol of the growing significance of leadership development. Chapter 6 examines the background to the opening of the College and notes the significance of its Leadership Development Framework, which helped to move the debate from the preparation of principals to a wider appreciation of the need to develop leaders at all levels and career stages. The many achievements of NCSL are discussed along with the various criticisms of its work.

Chapter 7 shifts the debate to developing countries. Their need for effective leadership is even greater than in rich Western nations but their resources are very limited. Pre-service preparation is rare and the limited development opportunities are mainly confined to in-service activity. Selection criteria are usually confined to teaching experience, while induction for new principals is limited and often inadequate. Ongoing support for school leaders is uneven and principals sometimes feel isolated and beleaguered. The chapter concludes with a recommendation that donor bodies give much more attention to school leadership preparation and development.

Chapter 8 examines the impact of leadership development. While its importance is widely acknowledged, specific evidence of its effects are limited. The chapter revisits the purposes of leadership development in order to determine criteria for evaluation. It assesses various models of evaluation and impact, and considers the emerging evidence that leadership preparation and development do make a difference to school and learning outcomes.

Chapter 9 provides an overview of this important issue. It claims that leadership matters and revisits the debate about content and process. It examines the relationship between leadership and values, and considers its implications for development. It outlines a model for school leadership development and concludes that preparation has been 'nationalised'.

I am grateful to the many people who have contributed to the development of this volume. David Middlewood has been a supportive series editor, and has provided many valuable suggestions on draft chapters. Derek Glover and I have worked together for many years and his literature reviews underpin much of the analysis in this book. I am also grateful for the more general support of many other colleagues in England and in many other countries. I have been fortunate to be able to conduct research in this field for several bodies, including the NCSL. Of course, the opinions expressed in this book are mine and may not represent the views of the College.

Finally, I wish to thank those close to me, especially Cha and Graham.

1

Leadership and school improvement

Introduction

There is great interest in educational leadership in the early part of the twenty-first century. This is because of the widespread belief that the quality of leadership makes a significant difference to school and student outcomes. In many parts of the world, including both developed and developing countries, there is recognition that schools require effective leaders and managers if they are to provide the best possible education for their students and learners. As the global economy gathers pace, more governments are realising that their main assets are their people and that remaining, or becoming, competitive depends increasingly on the development of a highly skilled workforce. This requires trained and committed teachers but they, in turn, need the leadership of highly effective principals with the support of other senior and middle managers.

Leadership or management?

Educational leadership and management are fields of study and practice concerned with the operation of schools and other educational organisations. Bolam (1999: 194) defines educational management as 'an executive function for carrying out agreed policy'. He differentiates management from educational leadership which has 'at its core the responsibility for policy formulation and, where appropriate, organisational transformation' (p. 194). Writing from an Indian perspective, Sapre (2002: 102) states that 'management is a set of activities directed towards efficient and effective utilisation of organisational resources in order to achieve organisational goals'.

Glatter (1979: 16) argues that management studies are concerned with 'the internal operation of educational institutions, and also with their relationships with their environment, that is, the communities in which they are set, and with the governing bodies to which they are formally responsible'. In other words, managers in schools and colleges have to engage with both internal and

1

external audiences in leading their institutions. This statement delineates the boundaries of educational management but leaves open questions about the nature of the subject.

The present author has argued consistently (for example, Bush 2003) that educational management has to be centrally concerned with the purpose or aims of education. These purposes or goals provide the crucial sense of direction, which should underpin the management of educational institutions. Management is directed at the achievement of certain educational objectives. Unless this link between purpose and management is clear and close, there is a danger of 'managerialism', 'a stress on procedures at the expense of educational purpose and values' (Bush 1999: 240). 'Management possesses no superordinate goals or values of its own. The pursuit of efficiency may be the mission statement of management – but this is efficiency in the achievement of objectives which others define' (Newman and Clarke 1994: 29).

Managing towards the achievement of educational aims is vital but these must be purposes agreed by the school and its community. If managers simply focus on implementing external initiatives, they risk becoming 'managerialist'. Successful management requires a clear link between aims, strategy and operational management.

The process of deciding on the aims of the organisation is at the heart of educational management. In some settings, aims are decided by the principal or headteacher, often working in association with senior colleagues and perhaps a small group of lay stakeholders. In many schools and colleges, however, goal setting is a corporate activity undertaken by formal bodies or informal groups. The school's aims are often encapsulated in a 'vision' or 'mission statement'.

School and college aims are inevitably influenced by pressures emanating from the wider educational environment and this leads to questions about the viability of school 'visions'. Many countries, including England and Wales, have a national curriculum and such government prescriptions leave little scope for schools to decide their own educational aims. Institutions may be left with the residual task of interpreting external imperatives rather than determining aims on the basis of their own assessment of student need.

Governments have the constitutional power to impose their will but successful innovations require the commitment of those who have to implement these changes. If teachers and leaders believe that an initiative is inappropriate for their children or students, they are unlikely to implement it with enthusiasm. Hence, governments would like schools to have visionary leadership as long as the visions do not depart in any significant way from government imperatives (Bush 2003).

Leadership

A central element in many definitions of leadership is that there is a process of influence.

Most definitions of leadership reflect the assumption that it involves a social influence process whereby intentional influence is exerted by one person [or group] over other people [or groups] to structure the activities and relationships in a group or organisation. (Yukl 2002: 3)

Leadership may be understood as 'influence' but this notion is neutral in that it does not explain or recommend what goals or actions should be sought through this process. However, certain alternative constructs of leadership focus on the need for leadership to be grounded in firm personal and professional values. Wasserberg (2000: 158), for example, claims that 'the primary role of any leader [is] the unification of people around key values'. Day et al.'s (2001) research in 12 'effective' schools in England and Wales concludes that 'good leaders are informed by and communicate clear sets of personal and educational values which represent their moral purposes for the school' (p. 53).

Vision is increasingly regarded as an essential component of effective leadership. Beare et al. (1992) draw on the work of Bennis and Nanus (1985) to articulate ten 'emerging generalisations' about leadership, four of which relate directly to vision:

1. Outstanding leaders have a vision for their organisations.
2. Vision must be communicated in a way which secures commitment among members of the organisation.
3. Communication of vision requires communication of meaning.
4. Attention should be given to institutionalising vision if leadership is to be successful.

These generalisations are essentially normative views about the centrality of vision for effective leadership. There is a high level of support for the notion of visionary leadership but Foreman's (1998) review of the concept shows that it remains highly problematic. Kouzes and Posner (1996: 24) say that 'inspiring a shared vision is the leadership practice with which [heads] felt most uncomfortable', while Fullan (1992: 83) adds that 'vision building is a highly sophisticated dynamic process which few organisations can sustain'.

It is evident that the articulation of a clear vision has the potential to develop schools but the empirical evidence of its effectiveness remains mixed. A wider concern relates to whether school leaders are able to develop a *specific* vision for their schools, given government influence on many aspects of curriculum and management.

Distinguishing educational leadership and management

The concepts of leadership and management overlap. Cuban (1988) provides one of the clearest distinctions between leadership and management. He links leadership with change, while management is seen as a maintenance activity. He also stresses the importance of both dimensions of organisational activity:

> By leadership, I mean influencing others' actions in achieving desirable ends. Leaders are people who shape the goals, motivations, and actions of others. Frequently they initiate change to reach existing and new goals ... Leadership ... takes ... much ingenuity, energy and skill. (p. xx)

> Managing is maintaining efficiently and effectively current organisational arrangements. While managing well often exhibits leadership skills, the overall function is toward maintenance rather than change. I prize both managing and leading and attach no special value to either since different settings and times call for varied responses. (p. xx)

Day et al.'s (2001) study of 12 'effective' schools leads to the discussion of several dilemmas in school leadership. One of these relates to management, which is linked to systems and 'paper', and leadership, which is perceived to be about the development of people. Bush (1998, 2003) links leadership to values or purpose while management relates to implementation or technical issues.

Leadership and management need to be given equal prominence if schools and colleges are to operate effectively and achieve their objectives. While a clear vision may be essential to establish the nature and direction of change, it is equally important to ensure that innovations are implemented efficiently and that the school's residual functions are carried out effectively while certain elements are undergoing change.

Decentralisation and self-management

Educational institutions operate within a legislative framework set down by national, provincial or state parliaments. One of the key aspects of such a framework is the degree of decentralisation in the educational system. Highly centralised systems tend to be bureaucratic and to allow little discretion to schools and local communities. Decentralised systems devolve significant powers to subordinate levels. Where such powers are devolved to the institutional level, we may speak of 'self-management'.

Lauglo (1997) links centralisation to bureaucracy and defines it as follows:

> Bureaucratic centralism implies concentrating in a central ('top') authority decision-making on a wide range of matters, leaving only tightly programmed routine implementation to lower levels in the organisation ... a ministry could make decisions in considerable detail as to aims and objectives, curricula and teaching materials to be used, prescribed methods,

appointments of staff and their job descriptions, admission of students, assessment and certification, finance and budgets, and inspection/evaluations to monitor performance. (Lauglo 1997: 3–4)

Lauglo (1997: 5) says that 'bureaucratic centralism is pervasive in many developing countries' and links this to both the former colonial rule and the emphasis on central planning by many post-colonial governments. Tanzania is one example of a former colonial country seeking to reduce the degree of centralisation (Babyegeya 2000).

Centralised systems are not confined to former colonial countries. Derouet (2000: 61) claims that France 'was the most centralised system in the world' in the 1960s and 1970s, while Fenech (1994: 131) states that Malta's educational system is 'highly centralised'. Bottery (1999: 119) notes that the UK education system 'has experienced a continued and intensified centralisation for the last 30 years'. In Greece, the public education system is characterised by centralisation and bureaucracy (Bush 2001).

Decentralisation involves a process of reducing the role of central government in planning and providing education. It can take many different forms:

Decentralisation in education means a shift in the authority distribution away from the central 'top' agency in the hierarchy of authority ... Different forms of decentralisation are diverse in their justifications and in what they imply for the distribution of authority. (Lauglo 1997: 3)

Where decentralisation is to the institutional level, for example in England and Wales, Australia, New Zealand, Hong Kong and South Africa, this leads to site-based management. 'A self-managing school is a school in a system of education where there has been significant and consistent *decentralisation* to the school level of authority to make decisions related to the allocation of resources' (Caldwell and Spinks 1992: 4, emphasis added).

The research on self-management in England and Wales (Bush et al. 1993; Levačic 1995; Thomas and Martin 1996) largely suggests that the shift towards school autonomy has been beneficial. These UK perspectives are consistent with much of the international evidence on self-management and the Organisation for Economic Co-operation and Development (OECD 1994) concludes that it is likely to be beneficial:

Greater autonomy in schools ... [leads] to greater effectiveness through greater flexibility in and therefore better use of resources; to professional development selected at school level; to more knowledgeable teachers and parents, so to better financial decisions, to whole school planning and implementation with priorities set on the basis of data about student [outcomes] and needs. (Quoted in Thomas and Martin 1996: 28)

Site-based management expands the role of school leaders because more deci-sions are located *within* schools rather than outside them. Autonomous schools and colleges may be regarded as potentially more efficient and effective but the quality of internal management is a significant variable influencing whether these potential benefits can be realised. Dellar's (1998) research in 30 secondary schools in Australia, for example, shows that 'site based' management was most successful where there was a positive school climate and the staff and stake-holders were involved in decision-making.

The significance of self-management for leadership development is that the scope for leadership and management is much greater. While managers in cen-tralised systems are largely confined to implementing policies and decisions made at higher levels in the bureaucracy, leaders of self-managing schools typ-ically have substantial responsibility for budgets, staff and external relations, as well as the interpretation and implementation of what is usually a prescribed curriculum. They necessarily have more opportunities for innovation than leaders working within a tightly constrained centralised framework.

The extra responsibilities mean that it is no longer sensible, if it ever was, to regard leadership as a singular activity carried out by the principal or head-teacher. Most self-managing schools now have an extensive leadership appara-tus, often including other senior managers (deputy and/or assistant principals) and middle managers (for example, heads of department or section). Young's (2006) study of large English primary schools, for example, shows an elaborate leadership pattern with large numbers of staff exercising leadership roles.

The growth in the number of leaders, and the scope of leadership, has led to developing interest in distributed leadership. As Harris (2004: 13) notes, it is 'currently in vogue'. However, she adds that it goes beyond formal roles to engage expertise wherever it exists within the organisation' (p. 13). The involvement of larger numbers of staff in educational leadership and manage-ment enhances the need for effective and appropriate development for leaders. This is the central focus of this book.

Leadership and school improvement

Leadership is often linked to school improvement. Almost two decades ago, Beare et al. stressed its importance:

> Outstanding leadership has invariably emerged as a key characteristic of outstanding schools. There can *no longer be doubt* that those seeking qual-ity in education must ensure its presence and that the development of potential leaders must be given high priority. (1992: 99, emphasis added)

This normative statement has been echoed by many other researchers, and by policy-makers. The establishment of the National College for School Leadership

(NCSL) in England is one significant example of the belief that effective leadership is vital for school improvement. The College's Leadership Development Framework repeats this mantra:

> The evidence on school effectiveness and school improvement during the last 15 years has consistently shown the *pivotal role* of school leaders in securing high quality provision and high standards ... effective leadership is a key to both continuous improvement and major system transformation. (NCSL 2001: 5, emphasis added)

Harris (2004: 11) reinforces this view by saying that 'effective leaders exercise an indirect but *powerful* influence on the effectiveness of the school and on the achievement of students' (emphasis added).

The relationship between the quality of leadership and school effectiveness has received global recognition. The Commonwealth Secretariat (1996), for example, referring to Africa, says that 'the head ... plays the most crucial role in ensuring school effectiveness'. The South African government's Task Team on Education Management Development also emphasises the importance of education management:

> The South African Schools Act places us firmly on the road to a school-based system of education management: schools will increasingly come to manage themselves. This implies a profound change in the culture and practice of schools. The extent to which schools are able to make the necessary change will depend largely on the nature and quality of their internal management. (Department of Education 1996: 28)

Huber's (2004a: 1–3) overview of leadership development programmes in 15 countries reaches a similar conclusion:

> The pivotal role of the school leader has been corroborated by findings of school effectiveness research for the last decades ... The research shows that schools classified as successful possess a competent and sound school leadership ... Studies on school development and improvement also emphasise the importance of school leaders.

This widespread belief that leadership and management are significant factors in determining school outcomes is not well supported by hard evidence of the extent and nature of school leadership effects. This issue receives extended consideration in Chapter 8 but it should be noted that Hallinger and Heck's (1998) widely accepted view is that school leadership effects account for about 3 to 5 per cent of the variation in student achievement. This is about one-quarter of all the effects attributable to school variables. The combination of limited size, and indirect impact, makes it difficult to detect leadership effects. While by no means negligible, such a small percentage effect raises questions about whether the rhetoric of school leadership ('no longer in doubt', pivotal role', 'powerful influence') is really justified. Although he was writing in the late 1970s, March's caution needs to be taken seriously almost three decades later:

> It is hard to show effects of organisation and administration on educational outcomes. Although there are some pieces of contrary evidence, the bulk of most studies and the burden of current belief is that little perceptible variation in schooling outcomes is attributable to the organisation or administration of schooling. (March 1978: 221)

The beliefs have changed, and there is now more 'contrary evidence', but much more needs to be understood about whether, to what extent, and how, leaders impact on school outcomes.

Conclusion

Effective leadership and management are increasingly regarded as essential if schools and colleges are to achieve the wide-ranging objectives set for them by their many stakeholders, notably the governments which provide most of the funding for public educational institutions. In an increasingly global economy, an educated workforce is vital to maintain and enhance competitiveness. Society expects schools, colleges and universities to prepare people for employment in a rapidly changing environment. Teachers, and their leaders and managers, are the people who are required to 'deliver' higher educational standards.

There is a widespread belief that raising standards of leadership and management is the key to improving schools. Increasingly, this is linked to the need to prepare and develop leaders for their demanding roles. While this is the main focus of this book, a prior question is the *nature* of leadership and management in schools. Which leadership behaviours are most likely to produce favourable school and learner outcomes? The next chapter examines the main models of school leadership and considers the evidence on their relative effectiveness in promoting school improvement.

2

Models of educational leadership

Introduction

In Chapter 1, we explored the research and literature linking educational leadership to school and student outcomes. We also noted the widespread belief that effective leadership is fundamental to successful schools and education systems. While there is an emerging consensus about the main constituents of leadership, there is much less clarity about which behaviours are most likely to produce the most favourable outcomes. Awareness of alternative approaches to leadership is essential in order to inform the design and development of programmes for aspiring and practising leaders. This chapter provides an overview of the main models of educational leadership and links them to similar models of educational management (Bush 2003; Bush and Glover 2003).

The implementation of the Education Reform Act (1988) and subsequent legislation in England and Wales, and similar moves towards self-management in many other countries, have led to an enhanced emphasis on the *practice* of educational leadership and management (Huber 2004a). Heads and principals are inundated with advice and exhortations from politicians, officials, academics and consultants, about how to lead and manage their schools and colleges. Many of these prescriptions are atheoretical in the sense that they are not underpinned by explicit values or concepts (Bush 1999, 2003). As we shall see later, however, governments may use conceptual language while shifting its meaning to support their own politically inspired intentions.

There is no single all-embracing theory of educational leadership. In part this reflects the astonishing diversity of educational institutions, ranging from small rural primary schools to very large universities and colleges, and across widely different international contexts. It relates also to the varied nature of the problems encountered in schools and colleges, which require different approaches and solutions. Above all, it reflects the multifaceted nature of theory in educational leadership and management. As a result, several perspectives may be valid simultaneously (Bush 2003).

9

The models discussed in this chapter should be regarded as alternative ways of portraying events. The existence of several different perspectives creates what Bolman and Deal (1997: 11) describe as 'conceptual pluralism: a jangling discord of multiple voices'. Each theory has something to offer in explaining behaviour and events in educational institutions. The perspectives favoured by managers, explicitly or implicitly, inevitably influence or determine decision-making. Morgan (1997: 4–5) uses 'metaphors' to explain the complex character of organisational life and notes that 'any theory or perspective that we bring to the study of organization and management, while capable of creating valuable insights, is also incomplete, biased and potentially misleading'.

The various theories of educational leadership and management reflect very different ways of understanding and interpreting events and behaviour in schools and colleges. They also represent what are often ideologically based, and certainly divergent, views about how educational institutions ought to be managed. Waite (2002: 66) refers to 'paradigm wars' in describing disagreements between academics holding different positions on theory and research in educational administration. The models discussed in this chapter are broad compilations of the main theories of educational leadership and management and are based on a systematic review of the literature and research (Bush 2003; Bush and Glover 2003).

Models of educational leadership and management

The present author has presented and classified theories of educational management for over 20 years (Bush 1986, 1995, 2003). This work categorises the main theories into six major models: formal, collegial, political, subjective, ambiguity and cultural (see Table 2.1).

Table 2.1 Typology of management and leadership models

Management model	Leadership model
Formal	Managerial
Collegial	Participative
	Transformational
	Interpersonal
Political	Transactional
Subjective	Postmodern
Ambiguity	Contingency
Cultural	Moral
	Instructional

Source: Bush 2003.

More recently, he has reviewed concepts of educational leadership, notably in work undertaken for the English National College for School Leadership (NCSL) (Bush and Glover 2003). As with educational management, the vast literature on leadership has generated a number of alternative, and competing, models. Some writers have sought to cluster these various conceptions into a number of broad themes or 'types'. The best known of these typologies is that by Leithwood et al. (1999), who identified six 'models' from their scrutiny of 121 articles in four international journals. Bush and Glover (2003) extended this typology to eight models. These are among the nine leadership models shown in Table 2.1, alongside the management models mentioned earlier in this chapter.

The rest of this chapter will examine these models and assess their significance for leadership practice in a wide range of educational contexts. While management models will also be discussed, the chapter will be structured using the nine leadership models featured in Table 2.1.

Managerial leadership

> Managerial leadership assumes that the focus of leaders ought to be on functions, tasks and behaviours and that if these functions are carried out competently the work of others in the organisation will be facilitated. Most approaches to managerial leadership also assume that the behaviour of organisational members is largely rational. Authority and influence are allocated to formal positions in proportion to the status of those positions in the organisational hierarchy. (Leithwood et al. 1999: 14)

This definition is remarkably close to that given for 'formal models' in the present author's trilogy of books on this topic (Bush 1986, 1995, 2003).

> Formal models assume that organizations are hierarchical systems in which managers use rational means to pursue agreed goals. Heads possess authority legitimized by their formal positions within the organization and are accountable to sponsoring bodies for the activities of their institutions. (Bush 2003: 37)

Dressler's (2001: 175) review of leadership in Charter schools in the USA shows the significance of managerial leadership: 'Traditionally, the principal's role has been clearly focused on management responsibilities'.

Caldwell (1992: 16–17) argues that managers and leaders of self-managing schools must be able to develop and implement a cyclical process involving seven managerial functions:

- Goal setting
- Needs identification
- Priority setting
- Planning
- Budgeting
- Implementing
- Evaluating.

It is significant to note that this type of leadership does not include the concept of vision, which is central to most leadership models. Managerial leadership is focused on managing existing activities successfully rather than visioning a better future for the school. This approach is very suitable for school leaders working in centralised systems as it prioritises the efficient implementation of external imperatives, notably those prescribed by higher levels in the hierarchy.

Bureaucracy, and by implication managerial leadership, is the preferred model for many education systems, including the Czech Republic (Svecova 2000), China (Bush et al. 1998), Greece (Kavouri and Ellis 1998), Israel (Gaziel 1998), Poland (Klus-Stanska and Olek 1998), South Africa (Sebakwane 1997), Slovenia (Becaj 1994) and much of South America (Newland 1995). Two of these authors point to some of the weaknesses of bureaucracy in education:

> The excessive centralisation and bureaucratisation, which continue to exist [in South America] in spite of the reforms undertaken, affect the efficiency of the system. (Newland 1995: 113)

> The Greek state should start moving towards restructuring the organisation of schools. Less complexity, formalisation and centralisation of the system, and more extended professionalism and autonomy of teachers and headteachers would be beneficial. (Kavouri and Ellis 1998: 106)

Managerial leadership has certain advantages, notably for bureaucratic systems, but there are difficulties in applying it too enthusiastically to schools and colleges because of the professional role of teachers. If teachers do not 'own' innovations but are simply required to implement externally imposed changes, they are likely to do so without enthusiasm, leading to possible failure (Bush 2003: 46).

Transformational leadership

Bush (2003) links three leadership models to his 'collegial' management model. The first of these is 'transformational leadership'.

This form of leadership assumes that the central focus of leadership ought to be the commitments and capacities of organisational members. Higher levels of personal commitment to organisational goals and greater capacities for accomplishing those goals are assumed to result in extra effort and greater productivity. (Leithwood et al. 1999: 9)

Leithwood (1994) conceptualises transformational leadership along eight dimensions:

- Building school vision
- Establishing school goals
- Providing intellectual stimulation
- Offering individualised support
- Modelling best practices and important organisational values
- Demonstrating high performance expectations
- Creating a productive school culture
- Developing structures to foster participation in school decisions.

Caldwell and Spinks (1992: 49–50) argue that transformational leadership is essential for autonomous schools: 'Transformational leaders succeed in gaining the commitment of followers to such a degree that ... higher levels of accomplishment become virtually a moral imperative. In our view a powerful capacity for transformational leadership is required for the successful transition to a system of self-managing schools.'

Leithwood's (1994) research suggests that there is some empirical support for the essentially normative transformational leadership model. He reports on seven quantitative studies and concludes that 'transformational leadership practices, considered as a composite construct, had significant direct and indirect effects on progress with school-restructuring initiatives and teacher-perceived student outcomes' (p. 506).

The transformational model is comprehensive in that it provides a normative approach to school leadership, which focuses primarily on the process by which leaders seek to influence school outcomes rather than on the nature or direction of those outcomes. However, it may also be criticised as being a vehicle for control over teachers and more likely to be accepted by the leader than the led (Chirichello 1999). Allix (2000) goes further and alleges that transformational leadership has the potential to become 'despotic' because of its strong, heroic and charismatic features. He believes that the leader's power ought to raise 'moral qualms' and serious doubts about its appropriateness for democratic organisations.

The contemporary policy climate within which schools have to operate also raises questions about the validity of the transformational model, despite its popularity in the literature. The English system increasingly requires school leaders to adhere to government prescriptions, which affect aims, curriculum content and pedagogy as well as values. There is 'a more centralised, more directed, and more controlled educational system [that] has dramatically reduced the possibility of realising a genuinely transformational education and leadership' (Bottery 2001: 215).

Transformational leadership is consistent with the collegial model in that it assumes that leaders and staff have shared values and common interests. When it works well, it has the potential to engage all stakeholders in the achievement of educational objectives. The aims of leaders and followers coalesce to such an extent that it may be realistic to assume a harmonious relationship and a genuine convergence leading to agreed decisions. When 'transformation' is a cloak for imposing leaders' or governments' values, then the process is political rather than collegial.

Participative leadership

> Participative leadership ... assumes that the decision-making processes of the group ought to be the central focus of the group. (Leithwood et al. 1999: 12).

This model is underpinned by three assumptions:

- Participation will increase school effectiveness.
- Participation is justified by democratic principles.
- In the context of site-based management, leadership is potentially available to any legitimate stakeholder.
  (Leithwood et al. 1999: 12).

Sergiovanni (1984: 13) points to the importance of a participative approach. This will succeed in 'bonding' staff together and in easing the pressures on school principals. 'The burdens of leadership will be less if leadership functions and roles are shared and if the concept of *leadership density* were to emerge as a viable replacement for principal leadership' (ibid. emphasis added).

Savery et al. (1992) demonstrate that deputy principals in Western Australia wish to participate in school decision-making although their desire to do so varied across different types of decision. They conclude that 'people are more likely to accept and implement decisions in which they have participated, particularly where these decisions relate directly to the individual's own job' (p. 24).

Interpersonal leadership

The third leadership model relevant to collegiality is the relatively new concept of interpersonal leadership. West-Burnham (2001: 1) argues that 'interpersonal intelligence is the vital medium'.

> Interpersonal intelligence is the authentic range of intuitive behaviours
> derived from sophisticated self-awareness, which facilitates effective
> engagement with others. (Ibid.: 2)

Interpersonal leadership links to collegiality in that it stresses the importance
of collaboration and interpersonal relationships (Tuohy and Coghlan 1997).
Bennett et al.'s (2000) research with nine English primary schools provides
evidence about the significance of interpersonal leadership and its
contribution to a collegial approach to school management:

> In four of the sample schools the headteacher was seen as leading from
> within the staff with strong interpersonal relationships. Here, staff inter-
> viewees referred to 'teams', 'friends working together' and 'certainty of
> consultation and support'. In this situation ... collegiality may be more
> readily achieved. (p. 347)

Transactional leadership

Bush (2003) links transactional leadership to the political model. Miller and
Miller (2001) contrast it with transformational leadership:

> Transactional leadership is leadership in which relationships with teachers
> are based upon an exchange for some valued resource. To the teacher,
> interaction between administrators and teachers is usually episodic, short-
> lived and limited to the exchange transaction. Transformational leader-
> ship is more potent and complex and occurs when one or more teachers
> engage with others in such a way that administrators and teachers raise
> one another to higher levels of commitment and dedication, motivation
> and morality. Through the transforming process, the motives of the leader
> and follower merge. (p. 182)

Miller and Miller's (2001) definition refers to transactional leadership as an
exchange process. Exchange is an established political strategy for members of
organisations. Heads and principals possess authority arising from their positions as the formal leaders of their institutions. They also hold power in the
form of key rewards such as promotion and references. However, the head
requires the co-operation of staff to secure the effective management of the
school. An exchange may secure benefits for both parties to the arrangement.
The major limitation of such a process is that it does not engage staff beyond
the immediate gains arising from the transaction. As Miller and Miller's definition implies, transactional leadership does not produce long-term commitment
to the values and vision being promoted by school leaders.

Postmodern leadership

Bush (2003: 127) notes that post-modern leadership aligns closely with his subjective model of management. It is a relatively recent model of leadership, which has no generally agreed definition. For example, Starratt's (2001) discussion of 'a postmodern theory of democratic leadership' (p. 347) does not define the concept beyond suggesting that postmodernism might legitimise the practice of democratic leadership in schools.

Keough and Tobin (2001: 2) say that 'current postmodern culture celebrates the multiplicity of subjective truths as defined by experience and revels in the loss of absolute authority'. They identify several key features of postmodernism:

- Language does not reflect reality.
- Reality does not exist; there are multiple realities.
- Any situation is open to multiple interpretations.
- Situations must be understood at local level with particular attention to diversity. (Ibid.: 11–13)

The postmodern model offers few clues to how leaders are expected to operate. This is also a weakness of the parallel subjective model. The most useful point to emerge from such analyses is that leaders should respect, and give attention to, the diverse and individual perspectives of stakeholders. They should also avoid reliance on the hierarchy because this concept has little meaning in such a fluid organisation. Starratt (2001) aligns postmodernity with democracy and advocates a 'more consultative, participatory, inclusionary stance' (p. 348), an approach which is consistent with participative leadership.

Sackney and Mitchell (2001: 13–14) also stress the centrality of individual interpretation of events while also criticising transformational leadership as potentially manipulative: 'Leaders must pay attention to the cultural and symbolic structure of meaning construed by individuals and groups ... postmodern theories of leadership take the focus off vision and place it squarely on voice.' Instead of a compelling vision articulated by leaders, there are multiple visions and diverse cultural meanings.

Moral leadership

This model assumes that the critical focus of leadership ought to be on the values, beliefs and ethics of leaders themselves. Authority and influence are to be derived from defensible conceptions of what is right or good (Leithwood et al. 1999: 10). Sergiovanni (1984: 10) says that 'excellent schools have central zones composed of values and beliefs that take on sacred or cultural characteristics'. Subsequently, he adds that 'administering' is a 'moral craft' (1991: 322). The moral dimension of leadership is based on 'normative rationality; rationality based on what we believe and what we consider to be good (ibid.: 326).

West-Burnham (1997) discusses two approaches to 'moral' leadership. The first he describes as 'spiritual' and relates to 'the recognition that many leaders possess what might be called "higher order" perspectives. These may well be … represented by a particular religious affiliation' (p. 239). Such leaders have a set of principles, which provide the basis of self-awareness.

West-Burnham's (1997) second category is 'moral confidence', the capacity to act in a way that is consistent with an ethical system and is consistent over time. The morally confident leader is someone who can:

- Demonstrate causal consistency between principle and practice
- Apply principles to new situations
- Create shared understanding and a common vocabulary
- Explain and justify decisions in moral terms
- Sustain principles over time
- Reinterpret and restate principles as necessary.
  (West-Burnham 1997: 241)

Gold et al.'s (2003) research in English primary, secondary and special schools provides some evidence about the nature of the values held and articulated by heads regarded as 'outstanding' by Office for Standards in Education (Ofsted) inspectors. These authors point to the inconsistency between 'the technicist and managerial view of school leadership operationalised by the Government's inspection regime' and the heads' focus on 'values, learning communities and shared leadership' (p. 127). These heads demonstrated certain values and beliefs through their words and deeds:

- Inclusivity
- Equal opportunities
- Equity or justice
- High expectations
- Engagement with stakeholders
- Co-operation
- Teamwork
- Commitment
- Understanding.

Gold et al. (2003: 136) conclude that their case study heads 'mediate the many externally-generated directives to ensure, as far as possible, that their take-up was consistent with what the school was trying to achieve'.

Sergiovanni (1991) argues that both moral and managerial leadership are required to develop a learning community:

> In the principalship the challenge of leadership is to make peace with two competing imperatives, the managerial and the moral. The two imperatives are unavoidable and the neglect of either creates problems. Schools must be run effectively if they are to survive ... But for the school to transform itself into an institution, a learning community must emerge ... [This] is the moral imperative that principals face. (p. 329)

Instructional leadership

Instructional leadership differs from the other models reviewed in this chapter because it focuses on the direction of influence, rather than its nature and source. The increasing emphasis on managing teaching and learning as the core activities of educational institutions has led to this approach being emphasised and endorsed, notably by the English NCSL (2001) which includes it as one of its 10 leadership propositions. Hallinger (1992a) argues that instructional leadership has been supplanted by transformational leadership in the USA, but these models are not seen as incompatible by NCSL.

Leithwood et al. (1999) point to the lack of explicit descriptions of instructional leadership in the literature and suggest that there may be different meanings of this concept. Southworth (2002: 79) says that 'instructional leadership ... is strongly concerned with teaching and learning, including the professional learning of teachers as well as student growth'. Bush and Glover's (2003) definition stresses the direction of the influence process:

> Instructional leadership focuses on teaching and learning and on the behaviour of teachers in working with students. Leaders' influence is targeted at student learning via teachers. The emphasis is on the direction and impact of influence rather than the influence process itself. (Bush and Glover 2003: 10)

Blase and Blase's (1998) research with 800 principals in American elementary, middle and high schools suggests that effective instructional leadership behaviour comprises three aspects:

• Talking with teachers (conferencing)
• Promoting teachers' professional growth
• Fostering teacher reflection.

Southworth's (2002) qualitative research with primary heads of small schools in

England and Wales shows that three strategies were particularly effective in improving teaching and learning:

- Modelling
- Monitoring
- Professional dialogue and discussion.

Southworth's third category confirms Blase and Blase's (1998) first point but his other strategies introduce new notions of which instructional leadership practices are likely to be successful. He also concurs with Hill (2001) that 'school leaders may lack sufficient knowledge of teaching and learning to provide adequate, let alone successful, instructional leadership' (Southworth 2002: 87) and advocates that this dimension should be included in leadership development programmes.

In contrast, Leithwood (1994: 499) claims that 'instructional leadership images are no longer adequate' because they are 'heavily classroom focused' and do not address 'second order changes ... [such as] organisation building' (p. 501). He adds that the instructional leadership image 'is now showing all the signs of a dying paradigm' (p. 502).

Despite these comments, instructional leadership is a very important dimension because it targets the school's central activities, teaching and learning. It may also be undergoing a renaissance in England, not least because of its specific endorsement by the NCSL (2001). However, this paradigm may be perceived as narrow because it underestimates other aspects of school life, such as socialisation, student welfare and self-esteem (Bush 2003: 16–17).

Contingent leadership

The models of leadership examined earlier in this chapter are all partial. They provide valid and helpful insights into one particular aspect of leadership. Some focus on the process by which influence is exerted while others emphasise one or more dimensions of leadership. However, none of these models provide a complete picture of school leadership. As Lambert (1995: 9) notes, there is 'no single best type'.

The contingent model provides an alternative approach, recognising the diverse nature of school contexts and the advantages of adapting leadership styles to the particular situation, rather than adopting a 'one size fits all' stance:

This approach assumes that what is important is how leaders respond to the unique organizational circumstances or problems ... there are wide variations in the contexts for leadership and that, to be effective, these contexts require different leadership responses ... individuals providing leadership, typically those in formal positions of authority, are capable of mastering a large repertoire of leadership practices. Their influence will depend, in large measure, on such mastery. (Leithwood et al. 1999: 15)

Yukl (2002: 234) adds that 'the managerial job is too complex and unpredictable to rely on a set of standardised responses to events. Effective leaders are continuously reading the situation and evaluating how to adapt their behaviour to it'. Leadership requires effective diagnosis of problems, followed by adopting the most appropriate response to the issue or situation (Morgan 1997). This reflexive approach is particularly important in periods of turbulence when leaders need to be able to assess the situation carefully and react as appropriate rather than relying on a standard leadership model.

Linking the models to leadership development

Leadership can be understood as a process of influence based on clear values and beliefs and leading to a 'vision' for the school. The vision is articulated by leaders who seek to gain the commitment of staff and stakeholders to the ideal of a better future for the school, its students and stakeholders.

Each of the leadership models discussed in this book is partial. They provide distinctive but unidimensional perspectives on school leadership. Sergiovanni (1984: 6) adds that much 'leadership theory and practice provides a limited view, dwelling excessively on some aspects of leadership to the virtual exclusion of others'.

The nine models, adapted from Leithwood et al. (1999) and Bush and Glover (2003), collectively suggest that concepts of school leadership are complex and diverse. They provide clear normative frameworks by which leadership can be understood but relatively weak empirical support for these constructs. They are also artificial distinctions, or 'ideal types', in that most successful leaders are likely to embody most or all of these approaches in their work (Bush 2003).

This analysis provides a starting point for linking the models to leadership development. Much depends on the nature of the leadership and management role in particular educational systems. If the principal's role is primarily about the implementation of policy determined outside the school, for example by national, provincial or local government, then leadership development should be primarily focused on developing 'managerial leadership'. This is the expectation in many developing countries and those in Eastern Europe.

Managerial leadership has been discredited and dismissed as limited and technicist but it is an essential component of successful leadership, ensuring the implementation of the school's vision and strategy. When vision and mission have been defined, and goals agreed, they have to be converted into strategic and operational management. The implementation phase of the decision process is just as crucial as the development of the school's vision. Management without vision is rightly criticised as 'managerialist' but vision without effective implementation is bound to lead to frustration. Managerial leadership is a vital part of the armoury of any successful principal (Bush 2003: 186).

A weakness of such an approach, however, is that it is rarely focused on the key task of managing teaching and learning and it does not require sustained engagement with school-level stakeholders. As a result, school and student outcomes may be disappointing and governments may become concerned about their inability to compete effectively in a global economy. This perception is reflected, for example, in the decision of the highly centralised Seychelles' government to require all their headteachers to acquire master's-level qualifications in educational leadership. It also influenced the report of the Task Team set up by the South African government shortly after the first democratic elections in 1994:

> Improving the quality of learning ... requires strategies which focus on change at the school and classroom levels ... Managers can no longer simply wait for instructions or decisions from government. The pace of change, and the need to be adaptable and responsive to local circumstances requires that managers develop new skills and ways of working. (Department of Education 1996: 13–14)

Improving the quality of learning requires an approach to leadership development, which focuses on 'instructional leadership'. This means attempting to change the mindset of leaders to regard the processes of teaching and learning as central to their role, rather than simply leaving such matters to classroom teachers. As we noted earlier, however, this model relates to the direction rather than the process of leadership. While encouraging leaders to focus on teaching and learning, it offers little guidance on how they should do so. 'It says little about the process by which instructional leadership is to be developed. It focuses on the "what" rather than the "how" of educational leadership. In this respect, it is a limited and partial model' (Bush 2003: 186).

To address the limitations of the instructional model, it makes sense to link it to an approach that addresses the process as well as the direction of leadership. Transformational leadership is currently in vogue as it accords closely with the present emphasis on vision as the central dimension of leadership. Successful leaders are expected to engage with staff and other stakeholders to produce higher levels of commitment to achieving the goals of the organisation which, in turn, are linked to the vision. As Miller and Miller (2001: 182) suggest, 'through the transforming process, the motives of the leader and follower merge'.

There is evidence to suggest that transformational leadership is effective in improving student outcomes (Leithwood 1994) but it may be manipulated to serve external requirements. In England, for example, the government uses the language of transformation but this is about the implementation of centrally determined policies not the identification of, and commitment to, school-level vision and goals.

Moral leadership has similar characteristics to transformational leadership in its emphasis on developing the commitment of followers, but its distinctive element is the focus on values and moral purpose. Leaders are expected to behave with integrity and to develop and support goals underpinned by explicit values. The main difficulty arises when staff or stakeholders do not support the values of leaders.

Participative leadership is likely to be effective in increasing the commitment of participants, and in the development of teamwork, but the price may be an increase in the time taken to reach agreement, and there may be difficulties for the formal leader, who remains accountable for decisions reached through the collective process. This model suggests that leadership preparation should focus on building consensus within the teaching team.

Interpersonal leadership also stresses the importance of collaboration, with staff, students and other stakeholders. Bennett et al.'s (2000) research with English primary schools suggests that this model can be effective in developing a conducive environment for learning and teamwork. This model suggests that leadership preparation should focus on building relationships with all stakeholders.

The transactional leadership model assumes that relationships with teachers and other stakeholders are based on a process of exchange. Leaders offer rewards or inducements to followers rather than seeking to improve their commitment or motivation, as in the transformational model. The main limitation of the transactional model is that the exchange is often short term and limited to the specific issue under discussion. It does not produce long-term commitment to the values and vision being promoted by school leaders. While a measure of exchange is inevitable for school leaders, it does not seem to be appropriate to include such approaches within leadership development programmes.

Postmodern leadership focuses on multiple individual perceptions. There is no absolute truth, only a set of individual insights. There are multiple visions and diverse cultural meanings instead of a single vision enunciated by leaders. The main limitation of this model is that it offers few guidelines for leadership action and development programmes can make use of it only by stressing the need to deal with people as individuals rather than as an undifferentiated group.

Contingent leadership acknowledges the diverse nature of school contexts and the advantages of adapting leadership styles to the particular situation, rather than adopting a 'one size fits all' stance. As Leithwood et al. (1999: 15) suggest, 'what is important is how leaders respond to the unique organizational

circumstances or problems'. The educational context is too complex and unpredictable for a single leadership approach to be adopted for all events and issues.
Given the turbulent environment, leaders need to be able to 'read' the situation
and adopt the most appropriate response.

Contingent leadership, then, is not a single model but represents a mode of
responsiveness, which requires effective diagnosis followed by careful selection
of the most appropriate leadership style. It is pragmatic rather than principled
and can be criticised for having no overt sense of the 'big picture'. In preparing
leaders, the focus should be on situational analysis and on careful adaptation
of leadership approaches to the specific event or situation.

The next chapter examines the rationale for leadership and management
development in education and the evidence that specific preparation is likely
to produce more confident and effective leaders.

3

The significance of leadership and management development

Introduction

In the previous chapters, we sought to explain why effective leadership and management are vital if schools and colleges are to be successful organisations, providing good learning environments for students and staff. We also showed that approaches to leadership are pluralist, with several different models being advocated and practised. The purpose of this chapter is to discuss the evidence that specific preparation is necessary if leaders are to operate effectively for the benefit of learners and the wider school community.

The case for specific preparation is linked to the evidence that the quality of leadership is vital for school improvement and student outcomes. Huber (2004a: 1–2), drawing on school effectiveness research, claims that 'schools classified as successful possess a competent and sound school leadership' and adds that 'failure often correlates with inadequate school leadership'. Leithwood et al. (2006: 4) show that 'school leadership is second only to classroom teaching as an influence on pupil learning'. Leadership explains about 5 to 7 per cent of the difference in pupil learning and achievement across schools, about one-quarter of the total difference across schools. These authors also note that there would be a 10 per cent increase in pupil tests scores arising from an average headteacher improving their demonstrated abilities across 21 leadership responsibilities. They conclude with this salutary statement:

> There is not a single documented case of a school successfully turning around its pupil achievement trajectory in the absence of talented leadership. (Leithwood et al. 2006: 5)

This powerful new evidence about the importance of school leadership contradicts the previous received wisdom that leadership made little impact on school outcomes. March (1978: 219), for example, claimed that 'any attempt to improve American education by changing its organisation or administration must begin with scepticism ... [they are] unlikely to produce dramatic or even perceptible results'.

Given the increasing body of evidence that leadership *does* make a difference, the spotlight turns to the issue of what preparation is required to develop appropriate leadership behaviours. This relates to conceptions of the principal's role. Traditionally, in many countries, school leaders begin their professional careers as teachers and progress to headship via a range of leadership tasks and roles, often described as 'middle management'. In many cases, principals continue to teach following their appointment, particularly in small primary schools. This leads to a widespread view that teaching is their main activity. Roeder and Schkutek (2003: 105) explain this perception in relation to one European country:

> So far a headteacher in Germany is seen as a primus inter pares, the teacher who takes care of the school as a whole along with his (reduced) teaching assignments. This role ... is strongly shaped along with pedagogical guidelines and closely connected to teaching.

This notion has the unsurprising corollary that a teaching qualification and teaching experience are often seen as the only requirements for school leadership. Bush and Oduro (2006: 362) note that 'throughout Africa, there is no formal requirement for principals to be trained as school managers. They are often appointed on the basis of a successful record as teachers with the implicit assumption that this provides a sufficient starting point for school leadership'. The picture is similar in many European countries, including Belarus, Cyprus, Denmark, Finland, Hungary, Iceland, the Netherlands, and Portugal (Watson 2003a). However, as Kitavi and van der Westhuizen (1997: 252) note in respect of Kenya, 'good teaching abilities are not necessarily an indication that the person appointed will be a capable educational manager'.

In the twenty-first century, there is a growing realisation that headship is a specialist occupation that requires specific preparation. The reasons for this paradigm shift include the following:

- The expansion of the role of school principal
- The increasing complexity of school contexts
- Recognition that preparation is a moral obligation
- Recognition that effective preparation and development make a difference.

These arguments are explored below.

The expanded role of school leaders

The additional responsibilities imposed on principals in many countries make great demands on post-holders, especially those embarking on the role for the first time. Walker and Qian (2006: 297) use dramatic imagery to stress the difficulties facing new principals.

> The rigours involved in the climb [to headship] ... accentuate during the first few years of the principalship. The energy previously needed to climb must be transformed into quickly balancing atop an equally tenuous surface – a spot requiring new knowledge, skills and understandings. In too many cases, the experience of the climb has done little to prepare beginning principals for the balancing act they are asked to perform.

The increased demands on school leaders emanate from two contrasting sources. First, the *accountability pressures* facing principals are immense and growing, in many countries. Governments, parents and the wider public expect a great deal from their schools and most of these expectations are transmitted via the principals. Crow (2006: 310), referring to the USA, points to enhanced societal demands within an 'increasingly high stakes policy environment':

> The higher expectations for US principals in the area of instructional leadership ... increased public scrutiny of public schools, and the promotion of privatisation as a public policy agenda, have significantly changed the role of school principal in the USA. US principals [also] work in a societal context that is more dynamic and complex that in the past. Changing student demographics, the knowledge explosion, the larger web of roles with which the principal interacts, and the pervasive influence of technology are a few features of this complex environment.

The pressures facing leaders in developing countries are even more onerous than those in the world's richest countries. In many countries in Africa, principals manage schools with poor buildings, little or no equipment, untrained teachers, lack of basic facilities such as water, power and sanitation, and learners who are often hungry (Bush and Oduro 2006). The Zambian education system, for example, is said to face 'wholesale systemic decay' (Harber and Davies 1997). Sapra (1991: 302) also notes the pressures arising from the 'phenomenal' expansion of the education system to fulfil the educational needs of the growing population in India.

The role of school principals is also expanding as a consequence of devolution in many countries.

Devolution to school level

One of the main global policy trends is the devolution of powers to site level.

In many countries, the scope of leadership and management has expanded as governments have shifted responsibilities from local, regional or national bureaucracies to school principals. This trend was noted in Australia as long ago as 1991. 'The control of many educational decisions is being transferred to schools ... and principals ... are being called upon to accept new responsibilities. Accordingly, politicians, management consultants, bureaucrats and educators alike are asserting the need for management training at all levels' (Johnson 1991: 275).

Brundrett et al. (2006: 89) make the same point in their comparative study of England and New Zealand. They say that the 'single largest change' in both countries has been the introduction of site-based management, linked to increasing accountability, leading to principals being positioned as 'the public face of the school' (ibid.: 90). Similar trends are evident in post-Socialist Eastern Europe. In the Czech republic, for example, schools have been given the opportunity to have their own resource management and significant freedom in staffing and pedagogic domains (Slavikova and Karabec 2003). Watson (2003b) notes that this is part of a Europe-wide trend, arising from the following circumstances:

• Increasing demands from local communities to have a greater say in the ways they are governed, notably in Eastern Europe
• A belief that exposure to market forces will raise standards.

Watson (2003b: 6) shows that devolution produces increasing complexity in the role of the head of the school and heightened tensions for principals: 'It leads to the need for the exercise of judgement in particular situations, rather then the simple following of rules.' We turn now to consider the extent and nature of this enhanced complexity.

The increasing complexity of school contexts

Hallinger (2001: 61) notes that 'the rapid change around the world is unprecedented'. This arises from global economic integration leading to widespread recognition that education holds the key to becoming, and remaining, competitive. Inevitably, this has led to increased accountability pressures, as we noted earlier. Because of the devolved nature of leadership in many education systems, these pressures are exerted on site-based leaders, notably school principals, who have to deal with increasing complexity and unremitting change. Huber (2004a: 4) makes a similar point, arguing that:

The school ... cannot any longer be regarded as simply imparting traditional knowledge within a fixed frame. Rather it is becoming an organisation which needs to renew itself continuously in order to take present and future needs into account. This imposes the necessity on school leadership to consider itself as a professional driving force and mediator for the development of the school towards a learning organisation.

Crow (2006: 315) notes the contribution of technological and demographic change to the complexity affecting school leaders. He comments that these changes must also impact on the nature of leadership preparation. One of the fastest changing societies is India and, 17 years ago, Sapra's (1991: 302) visionary analysis referred to the likelihood of increasing complexity driven by 'the educational needs of the growing population and increasing social demand for education, as well as to meet the requirements of trained manpower for the growing economy'. He adds that 'the success of educational managers to face these challenges with confidence will depend largely on the professional preparation that they will receive during the course of their career' (p. 308).

The pressures facing leaders in developing countries are particularly acute. The complexity they experience occurs across six dimensions:

- Many children do not receive education and many also drop out because of economic and social pressures.
- The economies of developing countries are fragile.
- Human and material resources are very limited.
- Many children and schools are scarred by violence.
- There is serious poverty in many countries and killer diseases, such as malaria and HIV/AIDs, are prevalent.
- There is widespread corruption and nepotism in many countries.
  (Bush and Oduro 2006; Harber and Davies 1997).

These contextual problems exert enormous pressure on school principals who are often 'overwhelmed by the task' (Commonwealth Secretariat 1996).

Leadership preparation as a moral obligation

The additional responsibilities imposed on school leaders, and the greater complexity of the external environment, increase the need for principals to receive effective preparation for their demanding role. Being qualified only for the very different job of classroom teacher is no longer appropriate. If this model was followed for other careers, surgeons would be trained as nurses and pilots as flight attendants. While competence as a teacher is necessary for school leaders, it is certainly not sufficient.

As this view has gained ground, it has led to the notion of 'entitlement' (Watson 2003b: 13). As professionals move from teaching to school leadership, there should be a right for them to be developed appropriately; a moral obligation. Requiring individuals to lead schools, which are often multimillion dollar businesses, manage staff and care for children, without specific preparation, may be seen as foolish, even reckless, as well as being manifestly unfair for the new incumbent.

The recent emphasis on moral leadership (Bush 2003: 170) suggests a need to move beyond the purely technical aspects of school management to an approach, which is underpinned by clearly articulated values and principles. If principals are expected to operate ethically, there is an equally strong moral case for them to receive specific preparation for their leadership and management roles. Watson's (2003b: 14) question about whether the employer has 'a professional or ethical obligation to develop headteachers' should be answered with a resounding 'yes'.

Effective leadership preparation makes a difference

The belief that specific preparation makes a difference to the quality of school leadership is underpinned by research on the experience of new principals. Sackney and Walker's (2006: 343) study of beginning principals in the USA found that they were not prepared for the pace of the job, the amount of time it took to complete tasks and the number of tasks required. They also felt unprepared for the loneliness of the position. Daresh and Male's (2000: 95) research with first-year principals in England and the USA identifies the 'culture shock' of moving into headship for the first time. 'Nothing could prepare the respondents, both American and British ... for the change of perceptions of others or for the intensity of the job'. Without effective preparation, many new principals 'flounder' (Sackney and Walker 2006: 344) as they attempt to juggle the competing demands of the post.

Brundrett et al. (2006: 90) argue that leadership development is a 'strategic necessity' because of the intensification of the principal's role. Evidence from Sweden (Stalhammer 1986 in Glatter 1991: 223) suggests a need for heads to develop their pedagogic outlook. 'Without a "compass", the head all too easily gets into difficult waters'.

Avolio (2005) makes a compelling case for leadership development based on the view that leaders are 'made not born'. Those who appear to have 'natural' leadership qualities acquired them through a learning process, leading Avolio (2005: 2) to deny that 'leadership is fixed at birth'. This leads to a view that systematic preparation, rather than inadvertent experience, is more likely to produce effective leaders.

Hallinger (2003a) stresses the importance of developing a carefully grounded relationship between leadership development, the quality of school leadership and both school and student outcomes. Earlier, his overview of research on school leadership development led to this cautious conclusion:

> Policymakers will be particularly keen to know if these training interventions *made a difference* in the practice of school leadership and school performance. Unfortunately, we cannot be sure since none of the studies were designed to address these questions … [We cannot] speak with confidence about the impact of the interventions on administrative practice in schools. (Hallinger 1992b: 308)

In the 15 years since this significant comment, evidence to support the value of leadership preparation has been slow to emerge. There is a widespread *belief* that it makes a difference. Lumby et al. (in press), for example, claim that 'leadership development actually makes a difference, be it in different ways, to what leaders do in schools'. However, empirical support for such assumptions is weak and usually indirect. Heck (2003) uses the twin concepts of professional and organisational socialisation as a lens to examine the impact of preparation. Professional socialisation includes formal preparation, where it occurs, and the early phases of professional practice. Organisational socialisation involves the process of becoming familiar with the specific context where leadership is practised. Leithwood et al. (1992) show that both dimensions of socialisation were helpful in contributing to principals' abilities to provide instructional leadership. Heck's (2003: 246) review of research in one US state shows that 'the socialisation process accounted for about one-fourth of the variance in administrative performance'.

Crow (2006: 321) suggests that 'a traditional notion of effective socialisation typically assumes a certain degree of conformity … a "role-taking" outcome where the new principal takes a role conception given by the school, district, university or community'. He argues that the greater complexity of leadership contexts requires a 'role-making' dimension, where new principals acquire the attributes to meet the dynamic nature of school contexts.

Bush et al.'s (2006b) evaluation of the National College for School Leadership 'New Visions' programme for early headship shows significant evidence of its impact on the 430 heads involved in the first two cohorts of the programme. Their survey results show high 'great help' ratings for four dimensions of personal development:

- Knowledge of educational leadership (48 per cent)
- Confidence (44 per cent)
- Coping with 'people' pressures (31 per cent)

- Ability to influence others (30 per cent).
  (Bush et al. 2006b: 193)

Bush et al. (2006b) also note perceived professional development benefits, including 'a clearer vision', 'a more democratic approach', being more 'inspiring and creative' and 'enthusiasm for learning'. The authors' school-based case studies show that all stakeholders perceive a shift to distributed leadership and a sharper focus on instructional leadership as a result of the New Visions experience (Bush et al. 2006b: 194–5).

Conclusion

Effective leadership is increasingly regarded as a vital component of successful organisations. The research shows that new principals experience great difficulty in adapting to the demands of the role. The process of professional and organisational socialisation is often uncomfortable as leaders adapt to the requirements of their new post. Developing the knowledge, attributes and skills required to lead effectively requires systematic preparation. Recognition of the importance of specific training and development has grown as the pressures on school principals have intensified. The greater complexity of school contexts, allied to the trend towards site-based management, has also heightened the need for preparation. There is also an acceptance of the moral basis for specific training and a growing body of evidence showing that preparation makes a difference to the quality of leadership and to school and pupil outcomes. In the next chapter, we examine the nature of leadership development programmes, including content and process.

4

The curriculum for leadership development: content and process

Introduction

In the previous chapter, we reviewed the evidence supporting the notion of specialist preparation for school leaders and managers. Just as teachers, doctors, lawyers and pilots, for example, need specific training, this also applies to school principals and other leaders. Appointing school leaders without such preparation is a gamble, and it is inappropriate to gamble when the 'losers' would be children or students. If this central case is accepted, the debate shifts to the nature of the development process. What should be the main components of leadership programmes?

Bush and Jackson's (2002) review of school leadership programmes in seven countries on four continents, for the NCSL, led them to conclude that the outline curriculum differed little despite the evident diversity in culture and context:

> The *content* of educational leadership programmes has considerable similarities in different countries, leading to a hypothesis that there is an international curriculum for school leadership preparation. Most courses focus on leadership, including vision, mission and transformational leadership, give prominence to issues of learning and teaching, often described as instructional leadership, and incorporate consideration of the main task areas of administration or management, such as human resources and professional development, finance, curriculum and external relations. (pp. 420–1, emphasis added)

Despite these similarities, however, these authors add that 'there are differences in the learning experienced by participants (ibid.: 421). Watson (2003b: 11) asks the key question; 'is training to be related to the needs of individuals, to those of the school or to the needs of the national system?' Where there is a mandatory or recommended qualification, as in England, Singapore and much of North America, it is inevitable that national needs have primacy. A national qualification requires a measure of consistency to reassure those recruiting leaders that all graduates have achieved at least threshold competence. However, Watson (2003b: 15) also points out that governments tend to favour skills-based programmes, which are more difficult to standardise than those focusing on knowledge and understanding.

Whether national, school or candidate needs are given primacy, the needs analysis process is vital. West-Burnham (1998) stresses its importance in determining the nature of leadership development: 'Needs analysis provides the crucial information to ensure that professional learning is appropriate, valid and relevant' (p. 99).

The NCSL's Leadership Programme for Serving Heads (LPSH) includes both 360-degree feedback and personal assessment to establish development needs for experienced heads. Similarly, the National Professional Qualification for Headship (NPQH) adopts a curriculum based around national standards which are used to identify the 'professional development needs of headteachers' (Male 2001: 464).

360-degree feedback is a diagnostic process that has become popular in leadership development programmes, including those presented by NCSL. This approach draws on the views of colleagues about the performance and development of leaders. Alimo-Metcalfe (1998), drawing on extensive empirical research, says that 360-degree feedback promotes self-awareness through 'a more accurate insight into one's own leadership behaviour ... related to one's performance and potential' (p. 37).

In the next section, we examine the *content* of leadership development programmes in different parts of the world. Subsequently, we explore the nature of the learning *process* for school leaders.

The content of leadership development programmes

Day (2001: 582) defines leadership development as 'expanding the collective capacity of organizational members to engage effectively in leadership roles and processes'. Bolam (1999: 196) argues that leadership development can be grouped into four modes:

- Knowledge for understanding
- Knowledge for action
- Improvement of practice
- Development of a reflexive mode.

Content-led programmes, particularly those provided by universities, may be regarded as predominantly aiming at 'knowledge for understanding'. Each programme has a 'curriculum' that gives an indication of the topics to be included. Chin (2003: 60) notes the 'diversity in the contents and methods of preparation programs' but adds that there is a 'general core of knowledge and skills', including the following:

- Strategies of communication and decision-making
- Legal aspects of school management
- Critical management tasks like strategic planning, total quality management and policy analysis
- School leadership both in instruction and administration
- Curriculum management and teaching methods
- Business management of financial and material resources
- External relationships with parents, education authorities and special interest groups
- Strategies of school evaluation of effectiveness and efficiency
- Strategies of school innovation and development.
  (Ibid: 61).

In the USA, the content is linked to the Standards for School Leaders, developed by the Interstate School Leaders Licensure Consortium (ISLLC). The ISLLC developed seven guiding principles 'to give meaning to the standards' (Murphy and Shipman 2003: 77). Standards should:

- Reflect the centrality of student learning
- Acknowledge the changing role of the school leader
- Recognise the collaborative nature of school leadership
- Upgrade the quality of the profession
- Inform performance-based systems of assessment and evaluation for school leaders
- Be integrated and coherent
- Be predicated on the concepts of access, opportunity and empowerment for all members of the school community.
  (Ibid.)

These principles provide a starting point for the construction of a curriculum. There are hundreds of university-based courses in the USA but Bjork and Murphy (2005) are able to offer a general guide to content:

> Most preparation programs have a similar program of studies that includes the following courses: curriculum, school law, finance, introduction to the principalship or superintendency, personnel management, managing buildings and facilities, research methods, human behaviour, school-community relationships (politics), educational governance and administration, educational psychology. (p. 14)

This is a daunting list of topics but these authors add that 'those programs tend to place greater emphasis on the application of knowledge to improve practice than on theoretical issues' (p. 15).

In Ontario, Canada, aspiring principals must take the Principals' Qualification Program (PQP). It has eight modules:

- Social context.
- Staff development and teacher supervision
- Management
- Leadership
- The school and its community
- Initiation of change
- Implementation of change
- Institutionalisation of change.
  (Huber and Leithwood 2004: 261)

European programmes vary significantly (Watson 2003b). In France, the national programme for school leaders of secondary schools has a similar content to that in the USA. It comprises:

> Administration, budgeting, school law, management techniques, teacher evaluation, interpersonal and communication skills, leading conferences and staff groups, assessment in practice [and] youth psychology. (Huber and Meuret 2004: 165)

French leaders take the national course following a selection process leading to an appointment as a deputy principal. Formal courses are thus supplemented by 'on-the-job' learning. 'Most trainees reckon that, while training sessions are important, their new experience as deputy heads teaches them essential aspects of their profession' (Fouquet 2006: 13).

The Finnish experience offers a contrast to the position in France, as leadership training is 'very decentralised' (Varri and Alava 2005: 8). University preparation programmes 'usually consist of educational leadership, educational policy-making and decision-making, educational administration, legislature and financing, the evaluation of education, and individual and organisational communication' (ibid.: 13), but the goals and content of other (non-university) programmes are very different.

Leadership development in Norway is focused on the university sector. Wales and Welle-Strand (2005) note that the following modules are given most focus in their programmes:

- Organisation and leadership
- Personnel leadership and budget administration

- Pedagogical leadership
- Law and public administration
- School development
- Quality and evaluation
- ICT and learning.
  (pp. 30–1)

In Austria, programmes are organised by each federal state. The programme in Salzburg includes five core modules:

- Communication and leadership
- Conflict management
- Lesson supervision
- School development
- School law and budgeting.
  (Huber and Schratz 2004: 203)

Singapore is a major centre for leadership development, the pioneer in Asia and one of the first countries to focus strongly on preparation for principals. The Ministry of Education, and the National Institute of Education, launched the Diploma in Educational Administration, a one-year full-time programme for prospective principals, as early as 1984 (Bush and Chew 1999). This was replaced by a new course, 'Leaders in Education', in 2001. Chong et al. (2003) stress that the 'delivery' is the main concern of the new programme but they also note the content of the modules:

- Managing competitive learning school organisations
- Marketing and strategic choice
- Applying new technology in managing learning
- Achieving excellence in teaching and learning
- Building human and intellectual capital
- Leadership for the new millennium
- Personal mastery and development for principals.
  (p. 170)

China has provided training programmes for principals for 50 years and more than 1 million had been trained by 1997. Daming (2003: 211) notes that 'most professional training programs continue to emphasise knowledge, and neglect administrative skills and leadership competencies' but offers few details of the content of such programmes. In contrast, there were no preparation programmes for principals in Taiwan before 2001 (Lin 2003). Subsequently, two principals' training centres were opened. The curriculum comprises 'fundamental' courses, such as research and organisational analysis, and 'professional' courses focusing on three areas:

- Instructional leadership
- Management and administration
- Politics and policy.
  (Lin 2003: 196)

South Africa's university sector has been presenting courses on educational management for many years and these often attract large numbers of participants. In 2007, the national Department of Education launched a new national qualification for principals, in partnership with many of the leading universities. The qualification is the Advanced Certificate in Education (ACE): School Leadership. The ACE is being piloted with 450 candidates at six universities in 2007–08 and is subject to a large-scale evaluation funded by the Zenex Foundation (Bush et al. 2007a). Subject to the findings of the evaluation, it may become mandatory for new principals from 2010. The ACE has 12 modules: two 'fundamental', six 'core' and four electives. These modules provide the content for the programme (see Table 4.1).

Table 4.1 Content of the South African ACE programme

Component	Module content
Fundamental	Language skills
Fundamental	Computer literacy
Core	Understanding school leadership and management in the South African context
Core	Managing teaching and learning
Core	Lead and manage people
Core	Manage organisational systems, physical and financial resources
Core	Manage policy, planning, school development and governance
Core	Develop a portfolio to demonstrate school management and leadership competence
Elective	Lead and manage subject areas/learning areas/phase
Elective	Mentor school managers and manage mentoring programmes in schools
Elective	Conduct outcomes-based assessment
Elective	Moderate assessment

Source: (Department of Education 2007)

Overview of leadership development content

This short description of leadership development programmes in nine countries provides a flavour of the content offered to principals and other leaders.

The discussion gives only an outline and does not reveal the details of these programmes or the ways in which they are delivered. However, it is possible to summarise the discussion and generate a 'model' for leadership development. Before doing so, it should be stressed that these programmes are context-specific so the use of a common 'headline' term may not mean that there is a shared curriculum. Rather they may be the starting point for different interpretations of leadership in diverse settings. Table 4.2 provides an overview of provision in nine of the 10 countries (the details of China's programmes are too limited to include in the table).

Table 4.2 shows that these programmes have several common topics, across national boundaries, but also some themes which appear to be context specific. Five of these appear in more than half the countries and might be regarded as the starting point for the creation of an international curriculum (Bush and Jackson 2002).

1. Instructional leadership

This topic relates to the core task of schools, promoting and developing teaching and learning. The descriptors vary and include pedagogical leadership, managing teaching and learning, and 'achieving excellence in teaching and learning'. 'Instructional leadership focuses on teaching and learning and on the behaviour of teachers in working with students. Leaders' influence is targeted at student learning via teachers' (Bush and Glover 2003: 10). As this definition implies, leaders impact on student learning indirectly. They seek to achieve good outcomes by influencing the motivation, commitment and capability of teachers. They also monitor and evaluate teaching and learning to check that high standards are being achieved. A course module on instructional leadership needs to address such themes.

2. Law

Schools operate within a specific legal framework and leaders must have regard to the law in enacting their roles. The purpose of a module on law is to ensure that leaders understand the main legal requirements affecting schools and their management.

3. Finance

This topic is particularly important for decentralised systems where there are self-managing schools. Principals may be responsible for substantial budgets and need the skills to set and manage budgets, audit spending and ensure that expenditure is targeted at meeting the school's objectives. They also need to provide financial statements to stakeholders, including school governing bodies.

Table 4.2 Content of leadership development programmes in nine countries

Topic	USA	Canada (Ontario)	France	Finland	Norway	Austria	Singapore	Taiwan	South Africa
Instructional leadership					✓	✓	✓	✓	✓
Management		✓	✓					✓	✓
Policy				✓				✓	✓
Curriculum	✓								
Law	✓		✓	✓	✓	✓			
Finance	✓		✓	✓		✓			✓
Managing people	✓	✓	✓		✓		✓		✓
Facilities management	✓								✓
Research methods	✓								
Community links	✓	✓							
Governance	✓								✓
Psychology	✓		✓						
Social context		✓							
Leadership		✓			✓	✓			✓
Managing links		✓							
Communication skills			✓	✓		✓			
Assessment			✓						✓
Administration			✓	✓	✓			✓	✓
Evaluation				✓	✓				
School development					✓	✓			✓
ICT and learning					✓		✓		✓
Conflict management						✓			
Marketing and strategic choice							✓		
Leadership development							✓		
Language skills									✓
Planning									✓
Mentoring									✓

4. Managing people

People are at the heart of any organisation and school leaders need to work through other people, staff and stakeholders, in order to achieve school objectives. In self-managing schools, leaders may be responsible for the full range of human resource management, including staff selection, induction, mentoring, staff development, deployment, performance appraisal, and discipline. These themes should be included in modules on managing people.

5. Administration

This term may denote routine management tasks, or refer to a wider and more significant set of processes. In some countries, the term 'management' may be used instead but the key point is that all schools have to carry out a range of administrative and managerial tasks in order to be functional. While courses need to reflect such processes, it is important to avoid 'managerialism', an emphasis on process at the expense of school goals. Administration should be regarded as a function that supports, not supplants, the educational purposes of the school.

While these five themes provide a starting point for the construction of a leadership development curriculum, attention needs to be paid to the delivery process. Significantly, in the twenty-first century, the emphasis has shifted from content to process, from 'what' is included in development programmes to 'how' they are designed and delivered. This is the focus of the next section.

Leadership development processes

School leaders are adults and need to be involved in determining their own learning needs. Tusting and Barton (2006) make two key points about adult learning:

1. Adults have their own motivations for learning. Learners build on their existing knowledge and experience. They fit learning into their own purposes and become engaged in it. People's purposes for learning are related to their real lives and the practices and roles they engage in outside the classroom.
2. Adults have a drive towards self-direction and towards becoming autonomous learners. Learning is initiated by the learner, and one role of the teacher is to provide a secure environment in which learning can take place.

They add that leadership development is moving away from the individual and prescribed towards the emergent and collective:

While the early research in management learning aimed to create a single rational framework for understanding the purposes, processes and effects of management education, training and development, in more recent years much more attention has been paid to the particular dynamics of the different contexts in which these processes are played out. (Tusting and Barton (2006: 40–1)

These characteristics appear to be consistent with an approach that allows for differing learning styles within a clear learning and organisational framework. This leads to a consideration of individualised learning.

Individualised learning

Burgoyne et al. (2004: 3) conclude that there is no single form of management and leadership capability that enhances performance in the same way in all situations, and no single way in which management and leadership development creates this capability. Rather, there are many different forms of development that can generate different types of management and leadership capability, which in turn can increase performance in various ways.

The individualisation of training is often appropriate but may be at the expense of the organisation. Proctor-Thomson (2005: 4) says that leadership development 'repeatedly reasserts the centrality of the individual leader' while James and Burgoyne (2001: 8) note that leadership development gives far more attention to individual leader development compared with the 'development of the constellation of leadership'. Hartley and Hinksman (2003) distinguish between 'leader development' and leadership development, saying that the latter should include a focus on structure, systems, people and social relations.

Individualisation becomes manifest through facilitation, mentoring, coaching and consultancy.

Facilitation

Rigg and Richards (2005) argue that support needs to be multifaceted (mentor, coach, facilitator) and bilingual (practitioner and academic). They show that facilitators in a number of public service leadership settings, including health and local government, play multiple roles:

- The facilitator of the process
- A source of subject expertise
- As mentor to participants.

They claim that facilitating is a craft, with multiple moments of judgement, and choices to be made. There are also manifold opportunities for facilitators to learn from experience and, like their participants, to gain insights from experimentation and reflection. They add that facilitators bring their own anxieties, impulses to control and responses to uncertainty, which influence the process of action learning as much as dynamics between the group participants (Rigg and Richards 2005: 202).

Facilitation is used extensively in NCSL programmes and is often one of the widely applauded dimensions of such programmes. It is particularly effective where the facilitators have specific knowledge of the contexts in which participants work. For example, facilitators who have experience of leading small primary schools are seen to have a deep understanding of the management issues facing such leaders (Bush et al. 2007b).

Mentoring

Mentoring refers to a process where one person provides individual support and challenge to another professional. The mentor may be a more experienced leader or the process may be peer mentoring. Bush et al. (2007b) note that mentoring is becoming more person centred with an increased awareness of the need to match mentor and mentee, to ensure that mentors are properly trained and that there is time, support and understanding of the reflective process. Hobson and Sharp's (2005) systematic review of the literature found that all major studies of formal mentoring programmes for new heads reported that such programmes have been effective, and that the mentoring of new heads can result in a range of perceived benefits for both mentees and mentors. Pocklington and Weindling (1996: 189) argue that 'mentoring offers a way of speeding up the process of transition to headship'.

Mathews (2003) argues that mentoring roles may be diverse, including those of guide, teacher, adviser, friend, tutor, catalyst, coach, consultant, role model and advocate. He concludes with cautions about the time required to make the process effective, and notes that mentoring relationships, particularly those which are cross-gender, may not be satisfactory.

Harrison et al. (2006) argue for a greater element of critical reflection for mentoring to be successful. Sundli (2007) challenges the 'cosy' conception of mentoring: 'Mentoring in the Norwegian instance shows a picture of an activity dominated by mentors' plans and values, and mentors' monologues in mentoring conversations with students' (p. 14).

Hawkey (2006) extends the argument for a new approach to mentoring through the use of appropriate language and understanding of emotional intelligence, so that there is empathy between mentor and mentee. Achinstein and Athanases (2006) suggest that mentoring fails where it is over-prescriptive and directive with only one right solution (p. 167). It is more likely to be successful where it is collaborative, investigative and transformative in nature.

Underhill (2006) examined mentoring research over the past 25 years to assess its effectiveness, and concluded that the overall mean effect size of mentoring was significant, indicating that mentoring does improve career outcomes for individuals. However, informal mentoring is shown to be more effective than formal programmes, echoing Herbohm's (2004: 393) finding that 'informal mentoring relationships benefit the protégé, the mentor and the employing organisation'.

The South African ACE: School Leadership programme gives a great deal of emphasis to mentoring. It is included as one of the 12 content modules but is also a key part of the delivery process. All participants have a mentor who works with a group of leaders in a 'network' (Bush et al. 2007a).

Singapore was a pioneer in the use of mentoring for aspiring heads on its Diploma in Educational Administration (DEA) programme. The new Leaders in Education programme involves allocating participants to schools for workplace learning, supported by the 'steward principal'. Chong et al. (2003: 169) say that this is intended to produce a 'profound learning experience for the participant'.

There is only limited evidence of the use of mentoring in Europe. Watson's (2003b) overview of provision in 24 European countries concludes that:

> Very few systems appear to be giving careful and systematic thought to how headteachers can be supported in their work in a way which leads to, rather than diminishes, professional skills, confidence and attitudes. It is in these contexts that peer support and mentoring can be of great importance to those involved. (p. 9)

Coaching

Coaching is in the ascendancy as a mode of development in NCSL programmes (Bush et al. 2007b). Davies (1996: 15) argues that coaching and supporting can be seen as the most effective management approach. Davies adds that coaching is 'a mutual conversation between manager and employee that follows a predictable process and leads to superior performance, commitment to sustained improvement, and positive relationships'.

Bassett (2001) states that coaching differs from mentoring because it stresses the skills development dimension. Bloom et al. (2005) add that coaches provide continuing support that is safe and confidential and has as its goal the nurturing of significant personal, professional, and institutional growth through a process that unfolds over time.

Simkins et al. (2006), looking at NCSL approaches, conclude that three important issues affect the coaching experience: coach skills and commitment, the time devoted to the process, and the place of coaching within broader school leadership development strategies. This connects with Leask and

Terrell's (1997) advocacy of coaching as a development mode for middle managers.

Coaching is a 'core element' of the programmes offered by the Centre for Excellence in Leadership (CEL), a body focused on leadership for the English Learning and Skills sector. The CEL says that 'this process works by reflecting and gaining insight, identifying what works, and acting on this learning. Coaching builds upon and acts on how managers work and learn' (www. centreforexcellence.org.uk).

Coaching is often regarded as an effective learning mode within leadership development programmes. Coaching, and mentoring and other forms of peer support, appear to work best when training is thorough and specific, when there is careful matching of coach and coachee, and when it is integral to the wider learning process (Bush et al. 2007b).

Consultancy

Consultants play a significant role in many NCSL programmes but this topic receives little attention in the leadership development literature. Referring to the English National Health Service (NHS), Hardy (in press) says that there are four core functions of consultant practice:

1. Expert clinical practice.
2. Professional leadership and consultancy.
3. Research and evaluation.
4. Education and professional development.

The CEL provides 'bespoke consultancy' and claims that it is 'critical to improving organisational performance'. It aims 'to work in a flexible and pragmatic way to further knowledge transfer and organisational capacity' (www.centreforexcellence.org.uk).

The NCSL includes 'consultant leadership' as one of five stages in its Leadership Development Framework (NCSL 2001). Its Development Programme for Consultant Leadership aims to encourage school leaders to take a prominent role in facilitating the learning of other leaders. The programme is framed around eight competencies:

• Accurate self-assessment; being aware of strengths and limitations
• Self-confidence; belief in one's own ability
• Self-management; ability to keep emotions in check
• Empathy; ability to sense others' feelings and concerns
• Partnering; ability to work collaboratively with others
• Pattern recognition; ability to identify patterns of behaviour
• Developing others; help others to develop their capabilities

- Non possessive warmth; caring for an individual without taking ownership. (www.ncsl.org.uk/programmes/dpcl/index.cfm)

Earley and Weindling (2006) draw on their NCSL evaluation of the London Leadership Strategy to examine what is known about 'consultant leaders'. They say that there are benefits for both parties and add that the relationship appears to work most readily with recently appointed heads. They point to the 'lonely and demanding job' of headship and conclude that 'the consultant leader's role of helping to provide ... support, together with the challenge needed to encourage development, is crucial' (p. 51).

E-learning

Personalised learning may also be achieved through e-learning. Chong et al. (2003: 165), referring to the Singapore context, say that information technology means that 'employees could have individualised learning programmes on demand'.

McFarlane et al.'s (2003: 7) review of the literature describes a range of indicators of effective practices in e-learning for leadership:

- Providing pre-programme diagnoses
- Optimising peer-to-peer and reciprocal learner-to-facilitator communications
- Encouraging a group dynamic to promote collaborative working within an e-learning environment
- Ensuring fast and reliable Internet connections
- Building in systems that guide or pressure learners to complete the programme
- Assessing e-learning activities so that they are an essential part of the programme.
- Ensuring that the programme has high status in the relevant community.

These points range from the technical ('fast and reliable Internet connections') to issues of design (ensuring that e-learning is integral to the learning process). Within NCSL programmes, online provision usually forms part of 'blended learning' but it often attracts a mixed or negative response. The evaluation evidence is consistent in attributing this to a range of technical problems, including design, slow speed, navigation and complexity, a lack of preference for this isolated mode of learning, and its lack of integration with other components of programmes (Bush et al. 2007b).

Group learning

Despite the tendency to emphasise individual leadership learning, group activities play a significant part in many development programmes. While this may sometimes be an opportunity for an essentially didactic approach, delivering a 'body of knowledge', there are several other group learning strategies that may be employed to promote participants' learning. The most important of these are discussed below.

Action learning

An enhanced focus on action learning arises, in part, because of an increased recognition that leadership and management are practical activities. While knowledge and understanding serve to underpin managerial performance, they provide an inadequate guide to action. Hallinger and Bridges (2007: 7) state that 'education in the professions should emphasise the application of knowledge' and add that professional development should aim at 'preparing managers for action' (p. 2).

Action learning is one example of this more practical approach. McGill and Beaty (1995) show that it provides for continuous learning and reflection by a 'set' of people, using an 'experiential learning cycle'. These authors show how action learning can contribute to management development through the development of the individual manager and the organisation as a whole (p. 209).

Smith (2001) focuses on the use of action learning in leadership development. Writing from a Canadian perspective, he states that action learning 'embodies an approach based on comrades in adversity learning from each other through discriminating questioning, fresh experience and reflective insight. It is a form of learning through experience ... based on the premise that we can only learn about work at work' (p. 35).

Action learning is a key dimension of NCSL's New Visions programme, for new first-time heads. Bush and Glover (2005: 232) note that 'this approach is perceived to be highly effective'. They cite the very positive views of one participant:

> The action learning sets are challenging: you have to explain your problems to others, they listen and discuss and finally feedback suggestions to alleviate your area of difficulty. (Ibid.)

Action learning is also an important part of the 'delivery architecture' in Singapore's 'Leaders in Education' programme. Chong et al. (2003: 169) explain the role of action learning:

> Participants know what they are taught, but they do not know what they will learn. They have to create their own knowledge through team learning, and this takes place in ... syndicates, a group of about six people meeting weekly and facilitated by a university professor. They know what knowledge they have created only when they come to the end of the programme.

Residential and off-site learning

Off-site learning is a central part of most leadership development programmes, involving periodic meetings at the provider's premises or at a conference centre. Bush et al. (2007b) note that most NCSL programmes make provision for off-site activity and evaluation evidence is generally positive but unspecific. Participants on several programmes appear to value such sessions because of their potential for networking but they also seem to provide space for reflection. Simkins et al.'s (2006) overview of NCSL programmes concludes that face-to-face activities were the 'most valued' aspect of all three core programmes: Leading from the Middle, NPQH and LPSH.

Networking and school visits

Residential and off-site learning provide the potential for networking. Inter-visitation and school visits, in particular, play a significant part in NCSL programmes. Bush and Glover (2004) advocate networking as one of four main leadership development approaches. Green (2001) suggests 'networking with peers' as one of five development modes, while James and Whiting (1998) advocate the provision of 'frameworks for networking' for deputy heads. Internships may be regarded as a specific form of networking and Crow (2001) argues that this may help with professional socialisation.

Bush et al.'s (2007b) overview of NCSL evaluations shows that networking is the most favoured mode of leadership learning. It is likely to be more effective when it is structured and has a clear purpose. Its main advantage is that it is 'live learning' and provides strong potential for ideas transfer. Visits with a clear purpose may also lead to powerful leadership learning. Visiting similar contexts (for example, other small primary schools) appears to be particularly valuable.

The South African ACE: School Leadership pilot programme places a lot of emphasis on 'cluster' learning. Participants are arranged in geographical groups to facilitate networking and collaborative learning (Bush et al. 2007a).

Singapore has a structured network, or partnership, comprising the National Institute of Education, schools and the Ministry of Education. Stott and Trafford (2000: 2) say that this partnership 'represents a shift away from the hierarchical to networks, from authority to influence'.

Portfolios

Portfolios are becoming significant elements of the assessment process in several leadership development programmes. Wolf and Gearheart's (1997) definition links portfolios to coaching and mentoring:

The structured documentary history of a carefully selected set of coached or mentored accomplishments, substantiated by samples of student work, and fully realised only through reflective writing, deliberation, and serious conversation. (p. 295)

Peterson and Kelley (2001) express reservations about teacher portfolios. Two of these are pertinent for leadership development:

1. They are difficult to use for judgements because of a lack of uniformity.
2. Teachers may not be objective when portfolios are used for summative purposes, particularly those related to career development.

Portfolios are a central element of the South African ACE: School Leadership programme. One of the core modules focuses on developing participants' portfolios and they are expected to produce 'a portfolio of practice evidence' as part of the assessment process. This approach was also used in the separate ACE programme operated, in the Gauteng province, by the Matthew Goniwe School of Leadership and Governance (MGSLG) in partnership with the University of Johannesburg. The mid-term evaluation of MGSLG (Bush et al. 2006d: 27) illustrates the point that portfolios are likely to vary considerably in quality and relevance. The researchers note that one of the 10 portfolios subject to scrutiny is 'an outstanding example of what should be expected of a student when submitting a portfolio'. They conclude that:

> This sample suggests that the bulk of the portfolios do not meet the standard required for an assessment tool, in terms of content or evidence of academic achievement. Only fifty percent of the sample linked their projects to the course content and some constituted a collection of documents without any real evidence to substantiate progress with the project. (Ibid.)

Despite this mixed evidence, portfolios have the potential to make an important contribution to candidates' learning, partly because programme assessment can be linked firmly to their schools, the context where leadership is practised.

Conclusion: content or process?

High-quality leadership is widely acknowledged to be one of the most important requirements for successful schools and school improvement (Bush and Jackson 2002; Harris 2003). However, there is ongoing debate about what forms of leadership development are most likely to produce effective leadership (Bush and Glover 2004; Bush et al. 2007b). The content of headship programmes varies according to the national context but there is a 'core' curriculum comprising five main themes:

- Instructional leadership
- Law
- Finance
- Managing people
- Administration.

In the twenty-first century, however, the emphasis has shifted from content to process. There is more attention to the facilitation of learning through approaches such as student-centred learning, action learning sets and open learning. The skills required of tutors are those of facilitation, coaching and mentoring. All these methods adopt a mix of support and challenge, and location along this continuum may be a more valid means of discriminating between approaches than relying on the label allocated to the activity.

There is extensive material on the use of different techniques in leadership development. What is less clear is how to combine these approaches to provide a holistic learning experience to meet the needs of leaders at different career stages, and in different contexts. Much of the research suggests that leadership development should go beyond *leader* development, through programmes and other interventions, to a wider focus on the school as an organisation. It is concerned with the ways in which attitudes are fostered, action empowered, and the learning organisation stimulated (Frost and Durrant 2002).

Bush et al. (2007b) identify four dimensions that should underpin the design of leadership development programmes:

The learning environment

The most successful learning experiences occur when there is a bridge between the work situation and the learning situation and where participants have the opportunity to reflect on their own practice, and then to share their response with others. Learning may be enhanced within the work situation, and through reflection, away from the normal context, but there are gains from opportunities to assess the contexts within which other participants work.

Learning styles

The most successful adult learning appears to grow from the identification of personalised learning needs. In the construction of programmes, much is to be gained from offering flexibility in content and approach. There should be opportunities for structured investigations, problem based learning, and reflective activities. There can also be considerable gains from understanding and developing the potential of e-learning.

Learning approaches

The literature shows that there is only limited value in didactic approaches and considerable gain from active learning. Wherever possible, learning objectives should be attainable through different means. In this respect there is a need to develop batteries of materials and approaches designed to present the same message(s) in different ways, including e-learning opportunities.

Learning support

There is evidence that people designated as tutors, mentors, coaches and facilitators may not understand their role and may have been selected on the basis that they are perceived to be, or to have been, successful leaders. To ensure effective support, there is a need for careful matching, and ongoing evaluation of relationships, and the quality of support (Bush et al. 2007b).

These four dimensions are normative constructs, the authors' views on how leadership learning can be enhanced through these four processes. However, in practice, much leadership and management development is content-led, with a knowledge-based curriculum. Bjork and Murphy (2005: 15), drawing on experience in the USA, provide a salutary comment on the contrast between the exciting potential for active learning and the prosaic reality of many leadership courses:

> Although convincing theoretical and empirical evidence support the use of active learning including simulations, case studies, practice-based and problem-based learning ... professor-centred rather than student oriented instructional strategies persist. Most courses are delivered using a lecture format that is viewed as being isolated, passive and sterile knowledge acquisition.

Finding an appropriate balance between content and process remains a very real challenge for those who design, and those who experience, leadership and management development programmes.

5

Preparing and supporting leaders in developed countries

Introduction

The purpose of this chapter is to assess the extent and nature of leadership preparation and development in developed economies. These include North America, most of Europe and several Asia Pacific countries, including Australia, New Zealand, Hong Kong and Singapore. Some of these countries, notably Canada, Singapore and the USA, were pioneers in the pre-service preparation of school principals while others, including much of Europe, were much slower to develop such programmes.

Many of these countries are among the richest in the world, as defined by gross domestic product (GDP) per head, and resource limitations are not a major constraint as they are in developing countries (see Chapter 7). Decisions about the extent and nature of leadership and management development are based on national judgements of need rather than being circumscribed by a lack of resources.

Leadership succession

In principle, there are two main strategies available to identify potential school leaders. First, those interested in such positions may be able to 'self-nominate' by applying for available posts and submitting themselves to the (stated or implicit) selection criteria. This approach is typically used by education systems with a high degree of decentralisation. The main limitation of this strategy is that insufficient well-qualified candidates may submit themselves for scrutiny. In England, for example, the imminent retirement of the post-war 'baby boom' era of school principals has generated widespread concern that there may not be enough replacements, leading to a national 'succession planning' initiative, led by the National College for School Leadership (www.ncsl.org.uk). The second strategy, typically used by centralised systems, is a planned approach, leading to central decisions about who should be considered for promotion. While this approach may be criticised on grounds of equal opportunity, it reduces the 'chance' element and provides the potential for smooth leadership succession. Watson (2003a: 7), referring to Europe, says that 'in most countries, headship posts are widely advertised as they become vacant. There are, however, still one or two systems where candidates are selected by the bureaucracy at municipal, regional or national levels and where there is no open competition for the post'.

Decentralised systems

As noted above, the notion of leadership 'succession' is more difficult to apply to decentralised systems. Because career development is the prerogative of the applicant, rather than the employer, it is not possible to adopt a planned approach. This is one element of the 'profound educational change' (Davis 2003: 145) arising from the redistribution of power from educational bureaucracies to individual school bodies. In England, the governing body of each school appoints its headteacher (Tomlinson 2003: 224). Similarly, the school board in Denmark conducts the selection process and makes a final recommendation to the municipal council. While appointing bodies can encourage applications, they cannot ensure that sufficient well-qualified candidates will apply (Moos 2003: 58).

One way of approaching this dilemma is for governments or other official bodies to create an appropriate leadership succession climate. England's NCSL is addressing this issue through its succession strategy. It cites Hargreaves and Fink's (2006) definition of succession planning; 'effective succession means having a plan and making plans to create positive and coordinated flows of leadership, across many years and numerous people' (NCSL 2006c: 5). It identifies four 'succession challenges' that need to be addressed as part of a coordinated strategy.

The retirement boom

The age profile of the profession, influenced by the post-war 'baby boom', means that a significant number of headteachers are likely to retire by 2009.

Perceptions of the job

The role of headteacher is perceived to be a difficult one and 43 per cent of deputy heads say that they do not want the top job.

A drawn out apprenticeship

Heads serve a long apprenticeship (on average 20 years) as teachers and deputies, before becoming headteachers. 'Making the route to the top swifter would render it more appealing to younger teachers' (NCSL 2006c: 7).

Regional variations

In certain parts of England, notably in inner London, it is very difficult to attract suitable candidates. Almost 50 per cent of schools need to re-advertise their headships in order to be able to make a good appointment. (NCSL 2006c)

These points also apply in certain other countries. The 'baby boom' affected many nations, perhaps particularly those in Europe, and the 'drawn out apprenticeship' is a factor in several education systems. As noted below, Cyprus and Malta both tend to appoint highly experienced teachers as heads. '[In Cyprus], the average age of principals on first appointment is around 55' (Pashiardis 2003: 36).

Centralised systems

In centralised systems, the bureaucracy is involved in defining criteria for leadership succession and in selecting candidates for preparation and/or preferment. The Singapore government, for example, identifies suitable teachers for promotion, as Chong et al. (2003) indicate:

> In the Singapore context, [leadership succession] has not been left to chance. The Ministry of Education has drawn up a framework where promising teachers are selected for various leadership or managerial positions in the school. Whilst most teachers remain in the classroom throughout their careers, those with leadership abilities may progress to other positions: senior teachers, subject heads, level heads and heads of department. (p. 167)

Several European countries follow a similar pattern. For example, in Belarus, 'vacant director [principal] posts are not usually advertised. Selection is normally made at the district level: potential directors are nominated by school or district authorities, interviewed and appointed by the district office. Some school districts operate a system whereby a "pool" or "reserve" of potential candidates are identified' (Zagoumennov and Shalkovich 2003: 18). In France, successful secondary school candidates are initially appointed as deputy headteachers and can be appointed to a post in any part of the country (Lafond and Helt 2003: 92).

One of the problems of such an approach is that it tends to reproduce the qualities of the existing group of principals. Gronn and Ribbins (2003) refer to 'ascriptive' systems, which tend to emphasise the personal characteristics of individuals and usually reproduce a leadership cohort (often predominantly male) from a narrow social base. Cyprus, for example, has adopted an approach that leads to the appointment of highly experienced, and usually male, principals (Gronn and Ribbins 2003; Pashiardis and Ribbins 2003).

Bezzina (2002: 10), referring to Malta, notes that most of his interviewees 'were promoted to principalship on the basis of seniority', and adds that 'none of the principals regarded themselves as working to a career plan designed to [lead] to a principalship position' (ibid.). This may be regarded as the inevitable consequence of top-down selection processes but it also reflects a reluctance to give up classroom teaching (ibid. p. 11). Bezzina (2002: 13–14) adds that political discrimination was previously an issue, as one of his respondents explains:

> The posts of deputy principals were very difficult to get because of the political atmosphere ... It was practically impossible if you had any connection with the Malta Union of Teachers (MUT) or if you were not particularly tied with the government party, then you wouldn't have any chance ... to get the post ... there were always a chosen few.

This factor is also prevalent in Cyprus. 'In order to be promoted, you have to belong to the correct political party' (Pashiardis 2003: 39). Similar considerations applied in Iceland until recently. 'The appointment of school principals was seen by many as having political considerations; i.e. the political majority hired principals "from the right party"' (Hansen 2003: 123).

Several countries in Eastern Europe are in the process of modifying what were previously highly centralised systems. In Estonia, headship appointments were previously dependent on membership of the Communist Party, which was also involved in the appointment. In the twenty-first century, posts are advertised and a committee recommends one of the short-listed candidates to the Municipal Council (Isok and Lilleorg 2003: 81). Similarly, the process has changed in Latvia since 1991. School directors are appointed by local education officials, following an open competition (Berzina 2003: 161). In Bulgaria, 'qualified applicants take part in a competition organised by a commission appointed by the employer' (Stanev and Mircheva 2003: 31).

In some countries, but by no means all, some form of preparation is required before appointment as a principal.

Leadership preparation

The notion of preparation suggests a preconceived orientation towards career

development, by the potential principals and/or system leaders. In many countries, aspiring principals must complete an approved pre-service qualification
before being considered for appointment. This focuses the attention of ambitious teachers who know what is required to progress towards senior leadership.
In other settings, there are no formal prerequisites except for the need to be
qualified and experienced teachers.

Formal preparation as a requirement for headship

One of the first countries to require a specialist leadership qualification for its
principals was Singapore, which introduced the Diploma in Educational
Administration (DEA) in July 1984 (Bush and Chew 1999). The National Institute
of Education received an annual intake of 50 vice-principals, selected and
sponsored by the Ministry of Education. The DEA was a full-time pre-service
programme, which included an internship of eight weeks at a mentoring principal's school. The mentors model their practice and also provide feedback to
the mentees on how they have handled a variety of school-generated tasks.
Bush and Chew (1999: 45) conclude that 'taken together, the internship
experience and management theory input acquired through coursework provides for a strong training background'. Chong et al. (2003: 168) add that the
DEA 'was known for its excellence in training school leaders'.

The DEA was replaced in 2001 by the 'Leaders in Education' programme
(LEP). The rationale for the change is explained by Chong et al. (2003):

> Whereas previously the compliant and efficient manager was valued in a
> system almost completely controlled from the centre ... the new educa-
> tional agenda demanded a new type of school leader who could cope
> proactively with a dynamic, complex and sometimes uncertain context.
> The old leadership thrived on conformity. The new leadership had to be
> ambitious and independent, innovative and able to succeed in conditions
> that were less clearly defined. (p. 168)

The main focus of the training is 'action learning'. Participants create their own
knowledge through team learning, and this takes place through 'syndicates', a
group of six participants meeting weekly, and facilitated by a university professor. They know what knowledge they have created only when they come to the
end of the programme (Chong et al. 2003).

School leader preparation has an even longer history in the USA. Brundrett
(2001) notes that it can be traced back to the nineteenth century and adds that
the USA is the nation that first formulated a theory of educational administra-

tion. By 1945, 125 institutions, mostly universities, offered courses in school leader training and many states then required the successful completion of such a programme before becoming principals or district supervisors (Huber 2004b). Bush and Jackson (2002) also note that most American states require aspiring principals to acquire an approved qualification, usually at master's level. Since 1994, providers in most states have adhered to the Interstate School Leadership Licensure Consortium (ISLLC) standards. These are intended to shift preparation and practice away from management towards leadership and to focus on improved student learning (Bjork and Murphy 2005). Preparation programmes generally include periods of 'clinical experience', to help in 'bridging the gap between the academic and practice arms of the profession' (ibid.: 8).

Similar arrangements are in place in Canada. In Ontario, for example, all aspiring leaders must complete the Principals' Qualification Programme (PQP) before being appointed as a principal or vice-principal (Bush and Jackson 2002). Candidates must follow 60 hours of practical experience, which involves taking a leadership role in their school, supervised by their principal. 'The practicum is intended to enable candidates to put [their] knowledge ... to the test in a real school setting and to conduct a leadership project independently' (Huber and Leithwood 2004: 261).

In France, there is a clear distinction between primary and secondary schools. There are no formal qualification programmes for primary headship but secondary leaders are expected to complete a comprehensive training programme. Aspiring leaders first take the 'concours', a four-hour written examination, followed by a presentation and an interview. Successful candidates then undertake a six-month qualification phase, comprising seminars, and internships in schools, the private sector and a public authority. The schools providing internships are selected according to the leadership qualities of the principal, who becomes the mentor for the aspiring head. Following this training, candidates are appointed to a school, often as a deputy head, for a two-year trial period. During this phase, there is further training tailored to the candidates' specific needs (Huber and Meuret 2004).

Bezzina (2002: 11) states that, in Malta, 'all prospective principals need to be in possession of a diploma in educational administration and management'. The need for preparation was taken seriously by most of his interviewees; 'you needed that kind of preparation and training and dialogue with your course colleagues' (p. 12). Significantly, though, the participants in his study regard their leadership experience as equally, if not more, valuable. 'Most principals spoke of their period as deputy principals as crucial to their professional growth' (ibid.).

In England, there is a statutory programme, the National Professional Qualification for Headship (NPQH). This was introduced in 1997 and will become mandatory for all first-time heads in 2009. It is underpinned by the National Standards for Headteachers (DfES 2004a). These are set out in six key areas:

- Shaping the future
- Leading learning and teaching
- Developing self and working with others
- Managing the organisation
- Securing accountability
- Strengthening the community.

The NPQH has three stages as follows:

1. Access; including induction, training and development.
2. Development; training, development and school-based assessment.
3. Final; 48 hours residential programme plus a final skills assessment.

Experienced leaders, for example deputy heads, may be able to proceed direct to the development or final stages without taking the preceding stage. Some applicants may have only 48 hours of 'training' before being awarded NPQH. Bush (2006) says that this shows the tension arising from a mandatory programme. It is vital to ensure that there are sufficient qualified applicants to enable school governing bodies to have a choice of potential headteachers. However, the drive for scale may be at the expense of quality:

> While requiring all heads to be qualified is a step forward, the NPQH makes only limited intellectual demands, and it is rare for any candidate to 'fail' (Bush 2006: 511).

The NPQH is under review during 2007. A fuller discussion of the work of the NCSL appears in Chapter 6.

In Estonia, school directors must have completed a school management course (240 hours) before being appointed. These programmes are offered by several higher education institutions (HEIs), via distance learning (Isok and Lilleorg 2003). Similarly, possession of a 'headship licence' is a legal requirement for appointment as a headteacher in Slovenia. The approved programme is provided by the National Leadership School and comprises six modules. Assessment is based on 'active participation and attendance, along with six satisfactory assignments' (Erculj 2003: 227).

South Africa is in the process of introducing a principals' qualification, the ACE: School Leadership, which is intended to become mandatory in 2010. It is being piloted in 2007–08 and the pilot has a comprehensive evaluation. The evaluation report will inform the Minister of Education's decision about whether to make the ACE a mandatory requirement for new principals. The pilot is being delivered by six universities but is primarily a practice-based qualification, with site-based assessment, local networking and mentoring by experienced principals (Bush et al. 2007a).

Optional headship preparation programmes

In many countries, leadership preparation programmes are available but are not a formal requirement for progression to headship. There is an emerging recognition of the importance of specific leadership learning but this has not progressed to the point where principals must undertake such preparation. Individual practitioners usually take the initiative to access such development opportunities.

Davis (2001) discusses the position in Victoria, Australia. He begins by noting that professionals and employers have both been reticent about giving a high priority to specific preparation for principals:

> I observe the reluctance of many school educators to appropriate personally their own belief in the efficacy of lifelong learning and to apply this belief to their own vocational circumstances. (p. 24)

> In Australia, the rhetoric about school improvement has almost always never been matched with the vocational training needed to produce the outcomes required. (p. 25)

Davis (2001) discusses the Australian Principals Centre, which has four categories of membership. One of these is the Associate Member, for affiliates who have completed pre-appointment training for the principalship. While this carries no formal status, Davis (2001: 28) believes that 'Associate Membership will provide members with a "competitive edge" when applying for jobs in the principalship'. This is evidently the main benefit of undertaking non-mandatory preparation but much depends on the attitudes of appointment panels to such accreditation.

In the Netherlands, training for school management was available as long ago as 1984 but formal qualifications are not required to become a school leader. However, Huber and Imants (2004: 145) note that 'school boards ... and the national government expect that ... teachers who aspire to become school leaders do take care for their professional preparation, and do take part in training sessions and courses'. There are several different preparation opportunities available to prospective principals.

Similar arrangements apply in Germany where all 16 states provide qualification programmes for new school leaders. Only five of these offer pre-service orientation courses. Huber and Rosenbusch (2004: 172) note that 'the assumption that a good teacher will automatically be a good school leader is still in existence. However, the significance of an adequate qualification is ... being more and more acknowledged by politicians and educators'.

In Hungary, there is no formal requirement for leadership training but there is a 'wide market of accredited programmes ... [and] school management masters degree programmes are very popular among ... deputies, prospective heads and teachers' (Gergely 2003: 112). Similarly, in Iceland, teaching qualifications and experience are the only formal requirements for principalship but 'teachers in management positions in schools have been entering a Graduate Diploma programme in school management ... in order to prepare themselves for school management' (Hansen 2003: 121).

Most of the countries featured in this section appear to recognise the importance of pre-service preparation for aspiring principals and many such leaders are accessing such opportunities. Elsewhere, however, there is little interest in formal leadership learning and apparent satisfaction with the existing arrangements. In Cyprus, for example, 'few [aspirant principals] engaged in substantial and proactive preparation' (Pashiardis and Ribbins 2003: 29). Those principals who have taken short courses were sceptical of their value, describing them as too 'theoretical' (ibid.). In practice, most had experienced an 'apprenticeship' model where they learned from working with 'good and supportive' (ibid.) principals. One woman principal, interviewed by Pashiardis and Ribbins (2003: 30), commented that 'in Cyprus, in education, there is really no such thing as preparing for the post'.

In Denmark, there are no national guidelines, formal expectations or competence objectives for educational leadership. There is no nationally run or certified education or training of aspiring school leaders. 'There seemed to be a consensus that leadership did not require any education beyond the initial training of teachers and perhaps some years of teaching' (Moos 2003: 60). There is now some discussion about a national leadership diploma course but this is conceived as a generic feature with all kinds of leaders, in the public and private sectors, taking the same programme.

The extent and nature of pre-service provision influence, to varying degrees, the selection of school principals.

Leadership selection

Centralised systems

The recruitment and appointment of school principals follows the 'succession' processes discussed above. In centralised systems, selection criteria are developed by senior personnel in the Ministry of Education or related bodies. In Cyprus, for example, teachers are appointed, located, transferred and promoted by the Educational Service Commission (ESC), an independent body appointed by the President (Pashiardis and Ribbins 2003: 14). The ESC supposedly has regard to three factors when choosing assistant principals and principals:

- Years of service
- Worth and excellence as a teacher
- Other diplomas, degrees or academic credentials.

Pashiardis and Ribbins (2003: 15) conclude that, as candidates have much the same academic qualifications, and because almost everyone is rated as an excellent teacher, the only significant differentiation comes from years in service. This leads to most secondary principals being appointed when over 50 years old. The United Nations Educational, Scientific, and Cultural Organization (UNESCO) national review of education on the island confirms that 'the principal criterion is age and seniority … competence in performing the work is scarcely taken into account' (Drake et al. 1997: 56–8). The review concludes that 'the system establishes what can only be described as a "gerontology in education" (ibid.: 58). The system also reinforces patriarchy with 68 per cent of secondary principals being men, despite women being in the majority in the teaching profession (Pashiardis and Ribbins 2003: 15).

In Singapore, successful completion of the 'Leaders in Education' programme is a requirement for aspiring principals but does not guarantee appointment. It is a necessary but insufficient condition for promotion. Appointments are made by the Ministry of Education on the basis of 'a standardised promotion procedure' (Huber and Gopinathan 2004: 225), informed by a performance appraisal grading system (Lim 2005: 75).

In Belarus, there are no formally stated criteria for selection and posts are not advertised. 'The selection is made on the basis of education officers' observation of the pedagogical, leadership and other aspects of the candidates' practice in their schools' (Zagoumennov and Shalkovich 2003: 18). The appointment of secondary school directors in Latvia requires the approval of the Ministry of Education and Science but local officials control the initial selection based on 'their understanding of what they need for the school' (Berzina 2003: 161). In the Czech Republic, headteachers are appointed by regional district offices, by agreement with municipalities. The selection process involves a panel comprising representatives of the region concerned, a teacher and a psychologist (Slavikova and Karabec 2003: 48).

In France, there is a national competition for aspiring secondary school principals. The personal files of applicants are scrutinised by a 'national jury' of inspectors and headteachers. About one-third of applicants are rejected at this stage. This is followed by an oral examination, conducted by inspectors, headteachers and private sector managers to assess candidates' motivation and capacity to be a leader (Lafond and Helt 2003: 91–2).

These examples illustrate the general principle that selection of school principals follows an essentially bureaucratic process. The degree of centralisation varies but decisions are made within national or local government, rather than by school-level bodies. The position is very different in self-managing schools.

Decentralised systems

In decentralised systems, the initiative usually lies with the candidate. Head-ships and other senior posts are advertised and there is an open competition for the posts. A shortlist of applicants is drawn up, ostensibly on the basis of a 'fit' between the candidates' qualifications and experience, and the job criteria. The final selection process usually involves a panel interview, often supplemented by practical activities, which may include teaching and/or managerial tasks. Increasingly, attention is paid to equal opportunities, to ensure, as far as possi-ble, that candidates are treated equally regardless of gender, race, disability and other personal variables (Bush and Middlewood 2005).

Watson (2003a: 7) reports that, in most European countries, 'headship posts are widely advertised as they become vacant'. He adds that there is 'wide vari-ety' in terms of who is involved in the selection process, ranging from national ministries, local government, parents and teachers. When the process is orches-trated by central government, as in Bulgaria (Stanev and Mircheva 2003), the degree of decentralisation is limited. While posts are advertised, the selection process is handled by the bureaucracy rather than by school-level panels. Where the selection is handled at local level, as in Estonia, school-level vari-ables may have greater prominence. Candidates are expected to articulate a 'vision' for the school to a temporary committee of five people, who make a rec-ommendation to the municipality's director of education (Isok and Lilleorg 2003: 80). In Iceland and Italy, however, the process is handled largely by municipal officials, with little school-level input (Hansen 2003: 120; Scurati 2003: 153). Rektors (principals) are also appointed by the municipality in Norway, usually on the basis of interviews (Lein 2003: 189).

Denmark is one of several European countries where the process is handled by the school board. It appoints a committee comprising representatives of par-ents, teachers and the senior management team. Following interviews, it rec-ommends a candidate to the full school board, which, in turn, makes a final recommendation to the municipal council (Moos 2003: 58). In Hungary, there is a substantial role for school-level bodies, including teachers and support staff, but the final decision is made by the local council (Gergely 2003: 110–11). In the 16 states of federal Germany, a preliminary selection is made by the local administration, following advertisements and the submission of documents by candidates. Several candidates are presented to school-level election bodies, which make the final decision (Roeder and Schkutek 2003: 100).

In England, the recruitment and selection processes are handled wholly at school level. The governing body appoints a panel, including parents, to carry out the selection procedure on its behalf. Shortlisted candidates are usually expected to make a presentation prior to interview. They may also be expected to undertake certain exercises and/or to teach a 'trial lesson' (Taylor and

Rowan 2003: 69). Principals are also appointed by school boards in Ireland (Murray 2003: 130), and the Netherlands (Derks 2003: 170).

New Zealand has one of the most devolved school systems in the world, and principals are appointed by individual Boards of Trustees. There is no formal requirement for aspiring principals to be qualified but a range of provision exists for candidates seeking to advance their claims and persuade Boards of their suitability (Huber and Robertson 2004: 249). There is a similar role for school boards in many North American states. Principals are appointed by the district but only on the advice of the school councils, which comprise local politicians, teachers, a pupil representative and parents. Only candidates with an approved master's degree in educational administration can be considered for appointment (Huber 2004b).

The selection process is at its most democratic in Portugal. Schools are managed by an Executive Council, 'a team of three teachers elected from the teaching body of the school by an electoral college which includes all teaching and non-teaching staff and parental and student representatives' (Afonso 2003: 196). Executive Council candidates must present themselves as a team and present their views about the school and its policies. Afonso (2003: 197) adds that the appointments are 'based on a political process carried out through voting procedures without the use of professional or technical procedures such as interviews, referees, curriculum vitae or psychometric tests'. Most candidates (90 per cent) do not have formal leadership qualifications.

Similar arrangements apply in Spain, except that the election is for a single school director rather than a leadership team. Applicants present their programme to the Administrative Council of the school, which may then question them. This process is followed by a secret ballot. Voting continues until one candidate has an absolute majority of the votes. Only teachers with a certificate of aptitude are eligible to apply. The certificate may be awarded following training and an evaluation by an inspector. Sala (2003: 236) concludes that the Spanish model is 'in crisis' because there are no applicants in 49 per cent of schools, and the school director has to be appointed by the community department of education.

Slovenia follows a similar pattern, with the School Council advertising the post and then leading the selection process. It has to seek the views of teachers and the local community, and the former are involved in voting, after attending candidates' presentations. The Ministry has to approve the appointment and will do so only if it is supported by a majority of the teaching staff (Erculj 2003: 226–7).

In all the school systems discussed above, judgements are made about the capability of candidates, by central or municipal government or by school-level bodies. In most cases, this takes account of their leadership qualifications and experience. In a minority of countries, only qualified candidates can be employed.

This candidate-led approach to staff selection has several advantages, notably enabling leaders who might be less favoured by appointing bodies, to advance their claims. However, Middlewood (1995) notes that such 'free market' approaches to recruitment also have disadvantages. In particular, when unsuccessful candidates make a further application, they have to start afresh without any accumulated 'credit' for their previous selection experience. In more centralised recruitment systems, the selectors are likely to build up a picture of all potential candidates which is much less readily available to school-level appointing bodies.

Regardless of their recruitment experience, new principals are likely to require induction into their new role.

Induction for leadership

Induction is the process by which new incumbents become familiar with the context in which they are leading, including the school culture. Crow (2006) distinguishes between professional socialisation (preparing to enter the profession) and organisational socialisation (learning how to lead in a particular context). All first-time principals need professional socialisation and, for many, there is the additional challenge of leading an unfamiliar school, meaning that organisational socialisation is also required. Bush and Middlewood (2005: 142) develop this notion to argue that induction has three main dimensions:

- Socialisation: enabling the new employee to become part of the organisation
- Achieving competent performance: enabling the new employee to contribute to the organisation effectively
- Understanding the culture: enabling the employee to appreciate the core values of the organisation.

Induction may be a deliberate process, with clear objectives and defined components, or an incidental activity, largely determined and orchestrated by the principal. Regardless of its nature, a learning process is inevitable, whether planned or unplanned.

Planned induction

The literature on leadership selection and preparation often gives little attention to induction but there are several examples of a formal process being offered to, or required of, newly appointed principals. In Helsinki, Finland, for example, there is 'a well-functioning' (Gayer 2003: 85) programme to train new principals. All incumbents assuming office attend a two-year training process containing aspects of municipal and national administration, occupational counselling, leadership training, educational management, organisational theory, economics and information technology (ibid.). In Sweden, the Induction Training Programme was introduced to help new principals in their first years of office. The main focus is on administration but principals should also be introduced to pedagogical leadership (Johansson 2003: 242). Similar arrangements have been proposed for Belarus (Zagoumennov and Shalkovich 2003) and Ireland (Murray 2003) but the extent of implementation is unclear. In Germany, some states offer 'further education' for newly appointed headteachers. 'This is designed to help them to get to know all those fields of work that differ from the tasks of teachers as soon as they have taken over their new role, inducting them into their new role' (Roeder and Schkutek 2003: 103).

The English NCSL introduced its Early Headship Provision (EHP), replacing the former Headship Induction Programme (HIP), in September 2006. There is an explicit rationale for this programme. 'It is clear to see that early headship represents a critical phase in any school leader's development' (www.ncsl.org.uk). The EHP is highly flexible and allows new heads to design their own learning pathways. The 'core' dimension of the EHP is the 'New Visions' programme. This is a process-rich offering that works through experiential learning. Independent evaluations of this programme have been exceptionally positive (Bush and Glover 2005; Bush et al. 2006b). New Visions is not compulsory but it is free to participants because NCSL wants a majority of new heads to take this innovative programme.

In New Zealand, there were no specific induction arrangements until the First Time Principals Programme was launched in April 2002. This involves three residential courses, two half-day school visits by mentors, e-community support and online learning. Brundrett et al. (2006: 98) note that the programme is neither compulsory nor a condition of appointment but comment that it represents 'a national determination to enhance the quality of leadership in schools' (ibid.).

There are similar arrangements in New South Wales, Australia, where the Principal Induction Program was introduced in 1997. This programme comprises four phases:

- A start-up conference, focusing on practical strategies for newly appointed principals
- Assignment to a colleague, who provides access to collegial networks
- District orientation, to familiarise principals with the operation of the district, and its support mechanisms
- A follow-up conference, focusing on theory and practice, establishing networks and providing access to experienced school leaders and to government officials. (Huber and Cuttance 2004: 242).

Unplanned induction

In several other countries, there is either a vague requirement to provide induction, or a voluntary arrangement available to, but not prescribed for, new principals. In Bulgaria, for example, 'the municipalities have an obligation to provide support' (Stanev and Mircheva 2003: 32) but the nature of this provision is unclear. Despite the isolation often felt by Hungarian principals, especially in rural areas, 'they often receive little support from maintaining authorities, which themselves lack educational expertise' (Gergely 2003: 114).

Where there is no formal provision, principals need to make their own induction arrangements. In the Netherlands, 'every new head starts his or her job with trial and error' (Derks 2003: 172) and often organise coaching, intervisitation or action learning sets to continue their leadership learning. Some Norwegian counties organise induction for school rektors but such provision is accessed on a voluntary basis only (Lein 2003: 187).

Where induction is absent or inadequate, principals' leadership behaviour is likely to depend on their previous experience. In Cyprus, Gronn and Ribbins (2003: 86) note that few principals 'found their formal induction to be satisfactory and soon they had to fall back on better-known examples of previous principals as their role models'.

Successful induction should smooth the path for new principals, accelerate their socialisation, enable them to make sense of the complex reality of school leadership and build their confidence to perform the role effectively. Inadequate or tacit induction is likely to slow down the learning process, and leave principals with a damaging sense of uncertainty about whether they are leading effectively or not. Where induction occurs, moreover, it may be regarded as a key stage in an ongoing process of continuing leadership development.

Leadership training and development

Leadership development is often the generic term used to describe any form of preparation or training for headship. In this section, we use it specifically to refer to activities undertaken *following* appointment as principal, that is, in-service training. Induction is one phase in this process but leadership development should be seen as any professional activity undertaken once principals have taken up their posts. Such provision may be seen as complementary to pre-service preparation or as a substitute for it. In Italy, for example, 'the lack of any initial preparation and training and the huge transformations that the headship has had to deal with in the last decades explain the outstanding development of in-service training initiatives. It is evident that these activities filled a crucial gap' (Scurati 2003: 153).

Leadership development arrangements are very diverse and reflect national contexts and imperatives. However, Watson (2003a: 9) points to one issue that seems to transcend national boundaries, at least in Europe:

> A continuing problem in many countries, however, is the identification of 'development' with 'training'. Too often, it appears, the development of headteachers is seen as being met through training courses alone, and little emphasis is given to other forms of professional development. It can readily be argued that opportunities to reflect upon one's experience, for job enrichment and job rotation, are also means of development.

Watson (2003a: 13–14) also asks two key questions about continuing leadership development:

* To what extent is training and development an entitlement for the individual?
* To what extent is it an obligation on the employer?

The notion of entitlement is implicit in the arrangements for earmarked funding for leadership development in Finland (Gayer 2003) and the Netherlands (Derks 2003). Finnish municipal departments earmark funding for professional development. In Helsinki, this amounts to approximately 1000 euros per principal per annum. Principals participate in advisory meetings, national conferences of heads of schools, seminars and international congresses (Gayer 2003: 86). There is also earmarked funding for English headteachers through the EHP programme discussed earlier. Participants have access to a 'flexible grant' of £1,300, which can be spent on a wide range of learning activities to meet their emerging needs (www.ncsl.org.uk/ehp). This is only available to practitioners in their first three years of headship but there is a strong case to extend this to all heads. An induction programme is also available for new principals in the English Learning and Skills sector (www.centreforexcellence.org.uk).

The notion of obligation is inherent in the arrangements for development in Belarus. It is a requirement that each school director undertakes formal training every five years, funded by central government and provided by institutes of education (Zagoumennov and Shalkovich 2003: 19). Similarly, French principals attend in-service training courses at regional or national levels. These are regarded as particularly useful when they change types of job or school, requiring adaptation to a new educational environment (Lafond and Helt 2003: 93).

Elsewhere in Europe, opportunities are less structured and depend largely on the individual initiative of principals. In Hungary, for example, there is a 'rich choice of programmes' but no focused development system for current heads (Gergely 2003: 113). There is little formal support in Estonia where the 'philosophy tends to be that it is up to the individual to rescue themselves if they are under the threat of professional "drowning"' (Isok and Lilleorg 2003: 81), implying that it is a remedial process. Similarly, in Slovenia, a laissez-faire approach is evident and principals are not required to 'refresh' their development. 'If they feel they should update their knowledge and skills they can attend in-service courses ... [but] no further training is formally required' (Erculj 2003: 228). Icelandic principals also need to take the initiative by applying for funded study leave while, in Norway, support is focused on 'updating' heads on national law and curricula, and on their role as school leader (Lein 2003: 190).

Bush and Jackson (2002) report on the study visits to leadership centres in seven countries, organised by the NCSL to inform its programme development. They note the availability of professional development for experienced principals in Sweden and in New South Wales, Australia. The Swedish programme is designed by the National Agency for Education and operates over three years, with residential sessions and in-school consultancy. The principal development programme in New South Wales is wide-ranging and leads to a Certificate of School Leadership and Management. It includes peer-assisted leadership, mentoring, coaching and shadowing, seminars and study leave. In contrast, experienced principals in the York District of Ontario, Canada, receive an annual professional development budget to spend on conferences or training (ibid.: 422).

In England, the NCSL has made provision for experienced heads since its inception. For much of the time, this was through the Leadership Programme for Serving Heads (LPSH). This offering has attracted large numbers of participants, with more than 7,000 heads having participated by 2001 (Collarbone 2001: 11). In 2007, this was replaced by the Head for the Future programme, available to any head with more than three years' experience. It 'is a fast paced and challenging blend of feedback, stimulating debate, demanding reflection and commitment to action' (www.ncsl.org.uk/programmes). A senior leaders' programme is also offered to College principals by the CEL (www.centreforexcellence.org.uk).

The NCSL is unusual in making extensive provision for experienced deputy and assistant heads, through the Established Leaders programme, and middle managers, via the Leading from the Middle programme. These are important stages in the College's Leadership Development Framework. These two products are offered through 'blended learning', giving more emphasis to practice and process than to theory and content. Evaluations for the NCSL suggest that these programmes are highly regarded by their participants (Bush et al. 2007b).

Singapore was the first country to make structured provision for middle managers, through what is now called the Diploma in Departmental Management (DDM). It is a 17-week full-time programme that enhances the capability of heads of department. Much of the programme focuses on departmental management, including instructional leadership, team management, and staff development and appraisal. Participants also visit schools in order to 'view exemplary departments in their own subject areas (Chong et al. 2003: 171).

All these examples demonstrate the diversity of in-service leadership development provision. However, they also illustrate the growing, if not yet universal, recognition that school leaders require continuing professional development. As Lam (2003: 187) suggests, in respect of Hong Kong, 'life-long education should be the basis for preventing professionals from becoming obsolete'.

Overview

Many of the countries featured in this chapter are among the richest in the world and could afford a 'Rolls Royce' model of leadership development. While there is widespread, and increasing, recognition that the nature of leadership and management are critical to enhancing the quality of teaching and learning, there is great diversity in the scope and shape of leadership development provision. These variations reflect different assumptions about the nature of schooling, the role of educational leaders and the place of formal programmes in developing school principals.

Several centralised systems have a planned approach to leadership succession, leaving little to chance, while decentralised countries leave the initiative to leaders, promoting equal opportunities but risking a shortfall in applicants. Demographic considerations, notably the imminent retirement of the 'baby boom' generation in Western Europe, and inadequate salary differentials in some countries, combine to create shortages of applicants, particularly in the less desirable locations.

There is growing recognition that leadership is a specialised profession, distinct from teaching, and requiring specific preparation. Several countries, notably England, Singapore, France, Estonia, Slovenia, Malta, and much of Canada and the USA, require aspirant principals to acquire a leadership qualification, although there is great diversity in the design and content of such programmes. However, many nations still appoint their principals on the basis of a teaching qualification and teaching experience alone without regard to their leadership knowledge and skills. Good leadership is an essential requirement for successful schools and this is too important to be left to chance.

Induction arrangements are also often inadequate, leaving principals to draw only on an ad hoc apprenticeship model, where they learn the job from their principals while holding a more junior leadership post. This can work well if the role model is competent, but it does not 'widen the lens' to allow aspirants to understand and experience alternative approaches. In any case, its effectiveness is random, depending on the quality of the leadership experience on offer in the aspirant's school. Even where this is good, it means that new leaders are likely to replicate previous practice rather than developing their own approach based on wider learning.

While many countries still do not require their leaders to have formal leadership qualifications, the debate has moved on in those countries where this argument has been won. There is now increasing recognition that leadership development is an ongoing process, beginning with middle managers, progressing through pre-service preparation for principals, and followed by induction and in-service development. This notion of continuing leadership development is exemplified by the NCSL's Leadership Development Framework. The next chapter examines the impact of what is the largest national leadership centre in the world.

6

The National College for School Leadership

Introduction

In the previous chapter, we reviewed the provision for leadership development in many developed countries in Europe, North America and the Asia Pacific. There is considerable diversity in the scale, nature and impact of the various models in use in these countries. We can assume that the pattern adopted in each nation reflects its collective sense of what is appropriate to underpin the quality of education in the twenty-first century. In evaluating these diverse approaches, we should acknowledge the vital importance of culture and context in shaping education, leadership and leadership development in each country. As the late Ray Bolam (2004: 251) explained, judgements cannot be made without an understanding of the history leading to contemporary policy choices:

> Models of preparatory training, certification, selection, assessment, induction and ongoing development for school leaders are necessarily rooted in specific national conditions and contexts. They are the product of unique, and dynamically changing, sets of circumstances – political, economic, social, cultural, historical, professional and technical – in that country.

This chapter focuses on these issues in one major European country, England. The analysis excludes Northern Ireland, Scotland and Wales, which have separate arrangements following the introduction of devolved powers during the past decade. The establishment of the English National College for School Leadership (NCSL) in November 2000 is probably the most significant global initiative for leadership development. Referring to the OECD study of nine countries (CERI 2001), Bolam (2004: 260) says that 'none of them match up to the college's unique combination of features'. Writing from a North American perspective, Crow (2004: 296) adds that the NCSL has the opportunity 'to be a driving force for world-class leadership in our schools and the wider community'.

The next section examines the historical background to the opening of the NCSL.

Leadership development in England before the NCSL

Bolam (2004: 251) says that the NCSL should be treated as 'the latest stage of an evolving policy innovation'. He attributes the evolving interest in school management to the introduction of comprehensive schools in the 1960s and 1970s. These were larger and more complex than the previous grammar and secondary modern schools, leading to an expansion of leadership roles and consideration of how schools should be managed. During the 1970s and 1980s, and very much on an ad hoc basis, courses were offered by local education authorities (LEAs), universities, and Her Majesty's Inspectorate (HMI). In 1983, the then Department of Education and Science (DES) established the National Development Centre for School Management Training (NDC) at the University of Bristol. University courses on school and college management became increasingly popular (Gunter 1997; Hughes et al. 1981).

The 1988 Education Reform Act located many more responsibilities at school level and greatly expanded the management role of headteachers and their senior colleagues. The government appointed a School Management Task Force (SMTF) in 1989 and its influential report (SMTF 1990) set the agenda for school management development for the next few years (Bush 2004). Probably its most important legacy was the establishment of mentoring schemes for new headteachers (Bolam et al. 1995; Bush and Coleman 1995; Southworth 1995).

The next major development was the establishment of the Teacher Training Agency (TTA), now the Training and Development Agency for Schools (TDA). The TTA took an interest in leadership and management development as well as the pre-service education of teachers. The TTA set up the National Professional Qualification for Headship (NPQH), the first national qualification for aspiring heads, in 1997. It also developed the HEADLAMP programme for new heads and the Leadership Programme for Serving Heads (LPSH), for experienced leaders (Bolam 2004; Bush 2004).

Bolam (2004) notes that the idea of a national college was discussed as early as the mid 1980s, but was rejected because it was felt that a residential college could not cope with the scale of need, with some 25,000 heads and up to 70,000 senior and middle managers. He argues that it returned to political prominence in the late 1990s, for three main reasons:

- It fitted the new Labour government's plans to raise standards in education.
- Developments in ICT meant that the residential dimension became less significant.

- The government was prepared to invest significantly in a national college and its ICT infrastructure.

Following a period of consultation, the NCSL opened in temporary accommodation on the University of Nottingham campus in November 2000. Former Prime Minister, Tony Blair, opened its state-of-the-art learning and conference centre in 2002.

The Leadership Development Framework

A distinctive, and enduring, feature of the NCSL is its Leadership Development Framework. This was conceptualised by the College 'Think Tank', chaired by David Hopkins, in 2001 (NCSL 2001). The Framework, which is under review in 2008, identifies five stages of leadership to inform programme development.

Emergent leadership

For teachers who are beginning to take on leadership and management responsibilities, including heads of subject/area and subject co-ordinators. Leading from the Middle is the main programme for this stage of leadership.

Established leadership

For experienced leaders who are not planning to pursue headship, including assistant and deputy headteachers. The Established Leader programme is the core offering in this category although this is likely to be replaced by Leadership Pathways.

Entry to headship

For those aspiring to their first headship and newly appointed first-time headteachers. Arguably, this stage comprises two distinct phases. The main programme for *aspiring heads* is the National Professional Qualification for Headship (NPQH). The main offering for *new heads* is the Early Headship Provision (EHP), incorporating the 'New Visions' programme.

Advanced leadership

For experienced headteachers looking to develop their professional qualities, skills and expertise. The main programme in this category is 'Head for the

Future', available to any head with more than three years' experience, which replaced the Leadership Programme for Serving Heads (LPSH) in 2007.

Consultant leadership

For experienced headteachers and other school leaders who are ready to further develop their facilitation, mentoring and coaching skills. The main provision for this stage is the Development Programme for Consultant Leadership (DPCL).

Beyond the Leadership Development Framework, the College also offers strategic programmes and provides for team development. *Strategic programmes* focus on issues within leadership or in particular types of schools. These include provision for school business managers, and Strategic Leadership of ICT (SLICT). *Team programmes* are for school leadership teams (SLTs) seeking to improve their effectiveness. These include Developing the Capacity for Sustained Improvement (DCSI) and Working Together for Success (WTfS) (www.ncsl.org.uk/programmes).

The NCSL claims that 'our Leadership Development Framework ... provides a coherent and flexible model for the development and support of school leaders, recognising the different strengths, needs and aspirations of leaders at all stages of their careers' (www.ncsl.org.uk/programmes). The framework is valuable partly because it goes beyond the previous focus on headship to acknowledge the distributed nature of school leadership, involving deputy and assistant heads, middle managers and business managers. It also shows the importance of lifelong learning for school leaders rather than focusing just on entry-level preparation, as in many other countries. In this sense, the framework is 'pioneering' (Crow 2004: 303).

This framework did not appeal to everyone. In 2001, David Hart, then secretary of the National Association of Head Teachers, criticised it for giving the impression that the college 'is attempting to rule the leadership world' and to be very prescriptive about how senior staff should improve their skills (cited in Mulford 2004: 315). The NCSL's Deputy Director rejects the notion of prescription but acknowledges that 'the college's development programmes are structured to help school leaders to progress through the framework for the benefit of their school and their own professional development' (Southworth 2004: 342). This impression is also confirmed by one aspect of the then Secretary of State's (David Blunkett's) remit letter. The College should 'provide a single national focus for school leadership development and research' (cited in Southworth 2004: 340). While a 'single national focus' might be regarded as a step towards unhealthy domination of the field in England, there is no doubt that the NCSL now operates a comprehensive suite of programmes to meet the needs of leaders at all levels. Male (2006: 72) notes that 'evaluations of the programmes and their impact consistently demonstrate high levels of satisfaction with outcomes, both at a personal and systemic level'. This was confirmed by a meta-analysis of 34 NCSL evaluations (Bush et al. 2007b).

The National Professional Qualification for Headship

The NPQH is the College's flagship programme and the only statutory part of its provision. As noted in Chapter 5, it is aimed at those leaders aspiring to headship. It was introduced by the TTA, now the TDA, in 1997 and is designed to establish leaders' suitability for headship. In this sense, it has always been more concerned with what leaders can do, than with what they know and understand. Leadership practice is perceived to be more important than an understanding of leadership theory and research.

The NPQH is progressing through two stages en route to mandatory status. From April 2004, new heads were expected to hold the qualification but there was a 'transitional arrangement allowing those with a place on the programme to be appointed to a first headship' (www.ncsl.org.uk/npqh). In practice, this often meant that headship applicants could be appointed if they promised to register for NPQH (Bush et al. 2007d). From April 2009, only those who have successfully completed NPQH will be able to be appointed to their first substantive headship position (www.ncsl.org.uk/npqh). Even this might be regarded as falling short of mandatory status, as it appears that school governing bodies will be able to make 'acting' appointments of candidates who do not hold the NPQH.

The NPQH has been through several iterations and was being redesigned as this chapter was being drafted (September 2007). Despite what the Secretary of State, in his 2007 remit letter, described as the 'good reputation of this flagship programme' (www.ncsl.org.uk/npqh), the NPQH has been subject to many criticisms. These can be summarised as:

- Being below the intellectual level required for such an important and complex role (Brundrett 2000; Brundrett et al. 2006; Bush 1998, 1999, 2006)
- Being 'too basic' or 'too easy' to obtain (Bush 2006; Bush et al. 2007)
- Being too reliant on a competency system (Brundrett 2000; Revell 1997)
- Having weak links with masters' level school leadership programmes (Bush 1998)
- Being based on a normative, and standardised, model of leadership (Brundrett et al. 2006).

The NCSL, in reviewing the qualification, identified five areas for improvement. The most significant of these are:

- Taking more account of candidates' personal, professional development needs
- Providing more opportunities to explore diverse school contexts
- Ensuring that graduation from headship signals immediate readiness for headship.

This final point was influenced by the college's Succession Planning initiative (see Chapter 5) and by statistics showing that only 43 per cent of NPQH graduates had achieved headship. The college's revised, and very ambitious, target is for 85 per cent of candidates to become heads on graduation (www.ncsl.org.uk/npqh).

The proposed model for the revised NPQH (www.ncsl.org.uk/npqh) continues the trend towards process-rich programmes discussed in Chapter 4. The model begins with a pre-entry stage, to stimulate interest in headship, and an assessment process to 'assess motivation, capability and readiness'. The application must be supported by the candidate's headteacher but this may become a barrier for some potential applicants. Black and minority ethnic (BME) candidates, for example, report that heads sometimes block their applications by saying that they are not ready for headship, a judgement which sometimes has racial overtones (Bush et al. 2007).

The development phase of the model may last from four to 12 months and is based around a personal development plan created by the 'trainee headteacher' and his/her coach. This individualised approach is consistent with the evaluation evidence (Bush et al. 2007b; Simkins, in press) and helps to address Brundrett et al.'s (2006: 99) criticism that the underlying assumption of NCSL programmes is that heads' 'professional development needs can be homogenised'. The components of this phase will be:

- NCSL materials
- Peer learning
- 'Coaching for improvement'
- Placement in another context (internship)
- Online activities
- Additional activities; personalised and determined locally. (www.ncsl.org.uk/npqh)

The assessment process will comprise a 'portfolio of evidence' and a panel interview to assess professional knowledge and understanding, leadership effectiveness and 'readiness for headship'. This latter point is critical in view of the optimistic assumption that 85 per cent of NPQH graduates will be ready for headship immediately following this assessment process. Given the succession planning pressures, there is a risk that panels will 'cut corners' to make sure that the supply of heads is sufficient to meet the increasing demand arising from demographic change.

The NPQH will soon become the only route to headship in England. This 'monopoly' position imposes great pressure on the NCSL to make sure it is 'fit for purpose'. A lack of pluralism provides a good prospect of a genuinely standardised qualification, in so far as this is possible with an individualised approach, but runs the risk of damaging the schools' system if it is inadequate. The new model addresses one of the criticisms above by requiring master's-level work as part of the assessment process. It also has the potential to meet the diverse needs of candidates through the intention to personalise development. However, there is a risk that it will become, or remain, un-demanding, to ensure that there is a sufficient supply of 'qualified' candidates. It also remains to be seen if it will contribute to improving standards of headship in England.

Strengths and achievements of the NCSL

The NCSL has been praised as an outstanding example of innovation in the preparation of educational leaders. It is a bold initiative that places leadership at the heart of the government's aim to raise educational standards. 'There can be little doubt that the college's overall conception, scale and execution represent a paradigm shift in comparison with predecessor models both internationally and in England and Wales (Bolam 2004: 260). It is certainly having a global impact, not least in the USA. For example, Levine (2005: 54) says that the NCSL 'proved to be the most promising model we saw, providing examples of good practice that educational administration programs might seek to emulate'. In South Africa, the Matthew Goniwe School of Leadership and Governance (MGSLG) was modelled to some extent on the NCSL, albeit on a much smaller scale and serving only a single province (Bush and Joubert 2004).

The NCSL has five main strengths:

- A national focus
- Programmes for different career stages
- An emphasis on practice
- Programmes underpinned by research
- Impressive reach and scale.

A national focus

The NCSL has substantial recurrent funding and is housed in a lavish purpose-built centre, leading Bolam (2004: 255) to claim that the NCSL now operates 'what is probably the most comprehensive and sophisticated *national* school leadership development model in the world' (original emphasis). The NCSL is one of only two national school leadership centres (Walker and Dimmock 2004: 271). (The other one, in Singapore, is much smaller.) Its influence goes well beyond that of any single university.

The advent of the NCSL was a major change from the previous ad hoc arrangements (Bolam 2004: 252), which ranged from a few days of induction by LEAs through to university master's and doctoral programmes. The NCSL provides the coherence that was missing in the previous arrangements and has moved leadership 'centre stage' in a powerful way. As Southworth (2004: 340) acknowledges, 'the scale and scope of the college's remit is considerable'. However, as we note later, national provision has limitations as well as strengths.

Programmes for different career stages

A distinctive feature of NCSL is its focus on school leadership at all levels. In creating a suite of development programmes, it has increased recognition that leadership goes well beyond headship (Southworth 2004: 341). As we noted earlier, this goal is encapsulated in its Leadership Development Framework, which comprises five stages, as well as in the development of strategic programmes and provision for school leadership teams. Southworth (2004: 341) claims that 'the framework was designed to provide a coherent and flexible model for the development and support of school leaders, recognising the different strengths, needs and aspirations of leaders at all stages of their careers'. Crow (2004: 303), from a North American perspective, adds that this wide provision 'should provide a useful framework for building leadership capacity across career stages in schools and contribute to international efforts in this regard'.

An emphasis on practice

The NCSL's programmes are underpinned by a desire to improve leadership *practice* in schools. This view is based on the Labour government's assumption that 'enhancing school leadership [is] a key driver of educational improvement' (Bush 2006: 509). This stance is illustrated by a focus on process rather than content, and on an approach to assessment that privileges what leaders can do, rather than what they know. As discussed earlier, the key phrase in assessing

NPQH candidates is 'readiness for headship' (www.ncsl.org.uk.npqh).

The NCSL's programmes include a wide range of activities thought to re
sent 'best practice'. Its international visits programme (Bush and Jackson 2
led senior College staff to conclude that process-rich strategies, such as n
toring, coaching, school visits, action learning and e-learning, are more li
to promote leadership learning than sustained engagement with theory
research. The author's evaluations (for example, Bush and Glover 2005; Bus
al. 2007b) show that networking, action learning, mentoring and coach
were rated highly by participants.

The NCSL also makes extensive use of current and recent school head
lead College provision. They work as tutors, mentors, coaches, facilitators
consultants on many NCSL programmes (Bush et al. 2007b). While the termi-
nology varies, the philosophy is consistent; current and recent headship
experience is regarded as vital to achieve successful socialisation of the new
generation of leaders. The new model NPQH, for example, 'requires serving
headteachers to give NPQH colleagues support, challenge and feedback'
(www.ncsl.org.uk/npqh). The programme will draw on the expertise of 'highly
effective headteachers' (ibid.) to provide placements, in coaching trainees, and
in serving on the graduation assessment panel. This stance is underpinned by
the view that contemporary experience of headship is essential to engage effectively with school leaders. The approach is generally facilitative rather than
didactic, drawing heavily on participants' experience. However, this approach
has several potential drawbacks, which we examine later in this chapter.

Programmes underpinned by research

The NCSL gives a high priority to research and publications. Its deputy director
is also director of research and the current incumbent, Geoff Southworth, is a
distinguished researcher, notably but not exclusively on primary headship. Its
research section plans and delivers the following activities:

- Programme evaluations
- Impact studies
- Practitioner research associateships
- Leading practice seminars
- Publications on leadership (180 identified on the College website).
  (www.ncsl.org.uk/research)

All major programmes are subject to external evaluation. Findings are usually
published and are regularly used to inform programme development. The College is increasingly concerned to assess the impact of leadership, and of its own

programmes, and several studies relate to this aim. One of the NCSL's most important achievements is the enhanced status given to practitioner research, notably through its research associateships (Bush 2004: 245; Coleman, 2007). Weindling (2004) found that the NCSL also funds more than half of school leadership research in England. Bolam (2004: 260) shows that the college's impact on research is immense:

> It is unquestionably taking research very seriously. Its director of research is a leading academic who has set out to promote evidence-informed practice, school-based enquiry and practitioner involvement in research. The basic aim is to produce and communicate findings that bring real benefit to school leaders.

Despite this impressive contribution to research on school leadership, Crow (2004: 301) adds a note of caution: 'The college may encounter the tension between leadership based on research and leadership based on acceptable policy. Although these do not have to be contradictory, they frequently collide in practice.' We explore this issue in the conclusion.

Impressive reach and scale

The NCSL has succeeded in involving many thousands of leaders in its various activities, a quantum leap in the scale of leadership development, reaching many more leaders than the universities, professional associations and local authorities in the pre-NCSL era. Coleman's (2005) survey shows that 47 per cent of England's 24,000 principals have taken part in one or more of the College's programmes while 85 per cent regard the NCSL as effective in promoting leadership development. The NPQH alone has 20,000 graduates and 2,800 candidates are expected to be registered on the programme in 2007–08. Seventy-three per cent of headteachers are regular visitors to the College's website (Male 2006: 71). However, some critics assert that the impressive scale is at the expense of quality and depth (Brundrett et al. 2006; Bush 2006). This claim is explored in the next section.

Weaknesses and limitations of the NCSL

Despite the considerable achievements of NCSL, and the significant boost it has given to school leadership, there remain certain doubts about whether its impact is wholly beneficial for the field in England. The main criticisms levelled at the College are:

- Only modest demands are made of programme participants.
- Its emphasis on practice is at the expense of theory and research.
- Its reliance on practitioners to lead programmes limits innovation.
- Its dominance of school leadership development is unhealthy.
- It is unduly influenced by the government.

Its demands are too modest

Instead of the sustained engagement with research and literature, expected in the best university courses, the College's expectations of participants are modest. Even the NPQH, the mandatory qualification for principalship, can be achieved by taking a 48-hours residential programme followed by a skills assessment, although this is set to change in 2008. The decision to require headteachers to acquire a specialist leadership qualification has been widely applauded but there are criticisms of the scope and nature of the NPQH. It is unambitious in that it requires limited engagement with theory and research and is focused primarily on applicants' perceived ability to do the job. It is evident that it is below the intellectual level regarded as necessary in North America (Bush 2004). The new model NPQH seems likely to provide a wider range of learning opportunities for 'trainee heads' but the nature of the content remains unclear. Other college offerings are not formally assessed so there is no straightforward way to judge the effectiveness of leadership learning despite the external evaluation programme (Bush et al. 2007b). Brundrett et al.'s (2006: 101) comment about the basic nature of NCSL provision requires serious attention:

> Questions remain as to how far the governmentally inspired leadership programmes have moved beyond the more reductivist elements of the competence paradigm towards educational programmes that develop the kind of reflective knowing and higher order cognitive abilities that will undoubtedly be required by leaders in the complex world of educational leadership in the 21st century.

The emphasis on practice is at the expense of theory and research

Levine (2005: 56) notes that the NCSL 'acts as a bridge between scholarship and practice, believing that research should drive practice and practice should fuel research'. However, the main emphasis is on participants' experience and NCSL programmes have been criticised for neglecting theory and research. University courses, in contrast, continue to be targeted at leaders at all levels and draw mainly on theory and research rather than participants' experience. They are aimed at enhancing participants' knowledge and understanding of school leadership rather than specific preparation for senior leadership roles, although many participants do become heads following such programmes (Bush 2006: 509). Brundrett et al. (2006: 103–4) argue that leadership programmes should not be 'isolated from the research, commentary and analysis of a wider educational constituency. If school leadership courses are to be successful they must integrate the best of academic programmes and take full account of emerging research evidence'. Southworth (2004: 351) claims that the college does learn from the wider leadership community, not least in commissioning research and evaluations, but the short-term nature of many programmes, and the extensive involvement of headteachers in delivery, leads to the inevitable conclusion that practice is regarded as more important than theory and research.

Its reliance on practitioners to lead programmes limits innovation

As we noted earlier, current and recent heads play important roles in the delivery of NCSL programmes. This seems set to increase with their heavy involvement in the new model NPQH. There is much to commend in this approach and it is used in many other countries, as we noted in Chapter 5, but it does have certain limitations. Crow (2004: 303–4) expresses concern about the 'conservative' nature of this approach:

> [Socialisation] involves newcomers being trained by veterans who pass on their knowledge and skills of the role. Many of the college's leadership development efforts involve veteran headteachers sharing their expertise and knowledge. This has also become a popular method in North American leadership development programmes … One question for reflection and research is whether the use of veterans encourages an innovative or custodial view of the role … If the goal of the learning is innovation and creativity, the issue of serial socialisation is not necessarily the most effective method.

Its dominance of school leadership development is unhealthy

Given its lavish funding, and its national profile, the NCSL has acquired an unhealthy domination of leadership development activities and an absolute monopoly of the statutory National Professional Qualification for Headship. From 2009, it will not be possible to become a headteacher without the NPQH.

University master's degrees, and other forms of leadership development, will not be acceptable alternatives. This will reinforce the perception, and the reality, that the NCSL is taking control of the school leadership agenda. 'The college's power has been exercised wisely but the lack of pluralism inevitably carries risks' (Bush 2006: 509).

A significant side-effect of the creation and success of the NCSL has been its negative impact on universities. Some have closed or scaled down their educational leadership centres while all are experiencing difficulties in recruiting candidates to their master's and doctoral programs. Many school leaders who might have taken postgraduate degrees now seem to believe that NCSL's less demanding provision is sufficient to meet their needs. The academic field of educational administration and leadership remains important for scholarship but its long-term future is uncertain. Some universities are responding by focusing on research, and international programmes, but these are unlikely to generate sufficient income to enable all the specialist centres to survive (Bush 2006: 510).

Levine (2005: 58) notes that the NCSL does not award degrees and adds that 'the college seeks partnerships with universities so that their students can earn degrees and credits for their NCSL work'. In practice, however, only a tiny proportion of College participants do so. The College's 2007 remit letter from the Secretary of State urges the College to consider how accreditation links with other courses might be developed (www.ncsl.org.uk/programmes). While the new model NPQH proposal makes tentative links to 'M'-level work, this falls short of the full articulation necessary to produce a meaningful link between College provision and academic leadership programmes.

It is unduly influenced by the government

When the NCSL was established, it was expected to fulfil three main roles:

- To be a government agency, responding to the requirements set out by the Secretary of State and elaborated by Departmental officials
- To be a voice for school leaders, articulating their views to government
- To be an independent organisation, developing and implementing its own policies and programmes.

While Southworth (2004: 340) states that the College seeks active partnerships with all the key players and stakeholders in the education service, there can be little doubt that NCSL's principal stakeholder is the government, for three main reasons:

1. It is a creature of government, which appoints its chair and governing body.
2. It operates in accordance with a remit letter produced annually by the Secretary of State.
3. It is funded on a substantial scale by government; more than £100 million per annum.
   (NCSL 2006b)

Levine (2005: 57) notes that 'juggling the three, sometimes inconsistent, roles of NCSL – government agency, independent organization, and voice of the schooling profession – is difficult'. While senior NCSL staff seek to find an appropriate balance, it seems inevitable that government requirements will be privileged as and when these constituencies come into conflict. This leads Thrupp (2005: 18) to argue that NCSL can be seen as 'the delivery arm of the DfES', rather than being an independent voice for school leaders. The 2006–09 Corporate Plan (NCSL 2006b: 27) states that 'we will continue to listen closely to school leaders'. Significantly, it adds that 'we are establishing a closer relationship with ministers and officials … and expect to have a stronger influence on future policy and practice' (ibid.). This shows the College's ambition to have a two-way relationship with government, responding to, but also influencing, policy. This is a sound strategy for both parties but it would be foolish to assume that this is an equal relationship. The NCSL's income, and its very survival, depend on satisfying the government's policy imperatives.

Conclusion

There are mixed views about the achievements and influence of NCSL. In its short life, it has fundamentally changed the landscape of leadership and management development by establishing a suite of impressive programmes, developing a notable electronic platform and becoming a major sponsor of school leadership research. The College's overall conception and scale represent a major step forward for school leadership and its development in England, and globally. The NCSL is unique in that it provides a national focus on leadership, stresses development at all stages, relies heavily on practice and practitioners, and reaches a very large number of school leaders. It is clear that it is now the dominant influence on school leadership development and research. However, the NCSL has also pursued scale at the expense of depth, demanded too little from its participants, and overemphasized practice at the expense of theory (Bush 2006: 508).

The future of the NCSL, as with any other government creature, depends on it retaining the goodwill and support of its stakeholders. School leaders, in particular, need to be satisfied that it meets their development needs in diverse and appropriate ways. The College does not take such support for granted, but seeks to find out leaders' views. This is done through formal surveys. For example the EduCom (2006) survey showed that 70 per cent of school leaders believe that the College's activities are effective (NCSL 2006b: 31). It also engages direct with leaders. The new Chief Executive met 2,000 school leaders during his first year in office.

Support from school leaders is essential but even more important is the relationship with government. The central issue here is likely to be perceived value for money, given the huge investment in infrastructure and programmes. One key dimension is the evidence of the impact of school leadership, and leadership development, on school and student outcomes. This is the focus of Chapter 8. Beyond this need for evidence is the wider requirement for ongoing political support. Bolam (2004) points to the problems of sustainability for publicly funded bodies such as the NCSL. The opposition Conservative Party pledged to abolish the NCSL had it been elected in 2005. While it seems secure following the re-election of the Labour Party, Bolam (2004: 263) cautions 'that nothing can, or should, be taken for granted'. The closure of the NCSL would be regrettable given its achievements but an even more serious concern is that much of the architecture of leadership development could be swept away with it. It is a measure of the College's success that it is not easy to visualise the leadership landscape without it.

7

Preparing and supporting leaders in developing countries

Introduction

Chapter 5 showed that school leaders face increasing demands and that these cannot be met effectively without initial, ongoing and specific preparation and development. However, these heads lead schools and colleges in what are generally favourable circumstances. Schools are usually well-equipped, teachers are suitably trained, and budgets are invariably adequate or good. A wholly different set of circumstances exists in developing countries. Leaders often work in poorly equipped schools with inadequately trained staff. There is rarely any formal leadership training and principals are appointed on the basis of their teaching record rather than their leadership potential. Induction and support are usually limited and principals have to adopt a pragmatic approach. Learners are often poor and hungry and may also be suffering the consequences of HIV/Aids (Bush and Oduro 2006: 359). In this chapter, we examine the challenges facing principals in developing countries, and explore the provision for leadership and management development for new and experienced school leaders.

The Commonwealth Secretariat (1996) has taken a keen interest in education in developing countries, and points to the difficulties of managing in such difficult contexts:

> The head ... plays the most crucial role in ensuring school effectiveness ... without the necessary skills, many heads are overwhelmed by the task.

Kitavi and van der Westhuizen (1997) refer to the problems experienced by school leaders in Kenya:

> Beginning principals in developing countries such as Kenya face problems that differ drastically from problems faced by their counterparts in developed countries such as the USA, UK and Australia ... The most serious problems facing beginning principals in developing countries like Africa

include: students who cannot pay school fees and buy books; shortage of school equipment; shortage of physical facilities; lack of staff accommodation; lack of playgrounds; students travelling long distances; and use of English as a medium of instruction. (p. 251)

These authors add that 'entering the principalship is an emotion-laden situation and the school principal is the key ingredient for success in school'. They note that little is known about school principals in developing countries and are critical of the current limited arrangements to support school leaders:

Despite the importance of the principalship, the means by which most principals in developing countries like Kenya are trained, selected, inducted and in-serviced are ill-suited to the development of effective and efficient school managers. (Kitavi and van der Westhuizen 1997: 251)

Oplatka (2004) provides a vivid description of developing countries:

These countries were ruled by Europeans for a long time, their economy is more agriculture-based, and they are usually characterised by high mortality rates, high birth rates, high levels of poverty and large gaps between rich and poor. (p. 428)

Bush et al. (in press) add that small island developing states (SIDS) suffer from similar problems, exacerbated by their small size. The main problems for such countries are:

- Geographical isolation, because of the distance from other countries
- Economic vulnerability, because of their dependence on a small range of economic activities
- Limited, or no, higher education provision, meaning that there is often no focal point for leadership development
- Limited natural and human resources.

Harber and Davies (1997) identify six dimensions in their overview of the educational context in developing countries:

- Demographic
- Economic
- Resource
- Violence
- Health
- Culture.

These elements are used to structure the discussion below, which also includes insights from other authors.

The demographic context

In many developing countries, some children do not receive education. According to the *Guardian* newspaper (28 June 2005), only 62 per cent of children were enrolled in primary education in 2001–02. The British Department for International Development (DfID) (www.dfid.gov.uk/mdg/education) presents a more optimistic picture, suggesting that 86 per cent of those in developing regions receive primary education, but this falls to 64 per cent in sub-Saharan Africa. In Ethiopia, the figure is only 40 per cent (Tekleselassie 2002). The problem is particularly acute for girls 'where the traditional view that a girl does not need an education to be a wife and mother still persists' (Harber and Davies 1997: 11). In most Ghanaian communities, parents following a traditional gender role stereotype still prefer educating their male children at the expense of the female child (Inkoom, 2005). As Brew-Ward (2002: 89) puts it, 'most parents have low aspirations for their daughters as far as academic endeavours are concerned. Most of them wish their daughters to marry and become good wives'. The DfID says that there has been good recent progress in girls' enrolment but gender gaps remain in sub-Saharan Africa and in South and West Asia (www.dfid.gov.uk/mdg/education).

The problem of low enrolment is exacerbated by high drop-out rates, caused by an inability to pay fees, and teenage pregnancy. In Ghana, rural headteachers encounter difficulty in obtaining fees from parents because most of them are peasant farmers and fishermen whose sources of income are seasonal. Failure of headteachers to collect fees promptly resulted in the Ghana Education Service (GES) laying an embargo on the payment of headteachers' monthly salaries (Oduro 2003: 125).

Drop-out rates are particularly high for girls. In Ghana, 84 per cent of males and 81 per cent of females attend primary school. Participation rates in secondary schools are 83.3 per cent for males and 76.8 per cent for females, a doubling of the gender gap (Girls' Education Unit 2002; Osei, 2003). Teenage pregnancy is linked to drop out in many countries. Bush et al. (2007a) report that up to 30 per cent of grade 12 girls in South Africa may become pregnant and leave school.

The economic context

Harber and Davies (1997: 12) point out that, in 1990, expenditure per student in OECD countries was 40 times that of countries in sub-Saharan Africa. 'The economies of developing countries are also particularly fragile and exposed to global economic changes'. In Ghana, as in many other African countries, child labour is often seen as a necessary evil for the survival of poor families (Agezo and Christian, 2002: 139). Principals are required to meet the needs of children who are often desperately poor (Bush et al. 2007a).

Small island developing states are dependent on a small range of economic activities, making them more vulnerable to 'terms of trade shocks' (Easterly and Kraay 2000: 2013). Campling and Rosalie (2006: 121) note that the transport costs associated with isolation 'act like a hidden tariff on trade'. They add that such vulnerabilities have a significant potential impact on public expenditure. Referring to the Seychelles, they say that 'contemporary levels of social welfare spending are probably unsustainable' (ibid.).

The resource context

Harber and Davies (1997) paint a bleak picture of the human and material resources available in developing countries. They refer to Lulat's (1988) view that the Zambian education system faces 'wholesale systemic decay'. They say that children in many developing countries have no text books while school buildings are often inadequate with overcrowded classrooms. In the Oyo State of Nigeria, Fabunmi and Adewale (2002 47) report that 'most secondary schools lack the basic educational resources that can make instruction effective and productive … Adequate furnished classrooms are often not available in schools … This accounts for classroom congestion in most secondary schools'. Similarly, Owolabi and Edzii (2000: 7) report that headmasters in Ghana who participated in their study 'confessed that they had quite insufficient quantities of books and stationery'.

Harber and Davies (1997: 15–16) add that, in parts of Sudan, 20 per cent of schools have no water and 57 per cent have no latrines. The majority of schools in rural areas in Africa do not have electricity. Schools often have to function with unqualified or under-qualified teachers. In 10 sub-Saharan countries, the majority of primary school teachers had not completed secondary education. Principals are expected to provide a suitable education with inadequate human and material resources.

Small island states often experience shortages of natural, financial and human resources. This has two significant implications for leadership development:

- There is a limited pool of candidates available to develop as school leaders.
- There is limited, if any, capacity to provide leadership development.
  (Bush et al., in press).

The context of violence

Many developing countries are plagued by war and violence, and children are often directly affected by the conflict. Women and children account for 92 per cent of war-related deaths in Africa (Harber and Davies 1997: 17). These problems often result in school closures.

The health context

Millions of people in developing countries live in absolute poverty. Thirty-three per cent of Africans are living with hunger (*Guardian* 28 June 2005) and 'children cannot learn effectively if they are weak from hunger' (Harber and Davies 1997: 19). Many children and teachers also suffer from killer diseases, including malaria and HIV/Aids. In Zambia, the number of primary school teachers who died from HIV/Aids in 2000, 'is equivalent to 45 percent of all teachers that were educated during that year' (Nilsson, 2003:16), while about 30 per cent of teachers in Malawi are reported infected (World Bank, 2002).

There is also the threat of drought in many countries, leading to malnutrition. In Niger, the Integrated Regional Information Network (IRIN) reports serious drought leading to a food crisis: 'Some 3.6 million people, including 800,000 children, are facing acute malnutrition, which at any moment could turn into a famine' (AlertNet 2005). Principals are leading schools that teach hungry children and serve deprived communities.

The cultural context

In developing countries, the values and beliefs of traditional cultures coexist, often uncomfortably, with imported Western ones. One example relates to the widespread corruption and nepotism in developing countries. Many teachers also have more than one job, leading to frequent absence and lateness. School management may also be affected by cultural politics. Oduro (2003: 203) notes that the management of Ghanaian schools is influenced by the 'Ghanaian cultural orientation towards the exercise of authority and power, the value for old age and language'.

This overview gives a flavour of the context within which school principals exercise their leadership roles. The situation is immensely difficult and challenging for many leaders in developing countries. They also rarely receive appropriate preparation for this demanding role.

Preparation for new principals

The notion of preparation suggests a preconceived orientation towards career development, by the potential principals and/or system leaders (Bush et al., in press). Consideration of this issue has two dimensions:

- The level of provision.
- The quality of provision.

Level of provision

In most developing countries, including small island states, there is no formal requirement for principals to be trained managers. They are often appointed on the basis of a successful record as teachers with an implicit assumption that this provides a sufficient starting point for school leadership (Bush and Oduro 2006: 362). This problem is not confined to developing countries, as we noted in Chapter 5. Given the demanding contexts mentioned earlier, however, the lack of training is likely to have particularly serious consequences. Simkins et al. (1998: 131), referring to Pakistan, say that 'management training and development might help to improve the effectiveness of head teachers'.

In Kenya, 'deputy principals as well as good assistant teachers are appointed to the principalship without any leadership training ... good teaching abilities are not necessarily an indication that the person appointed will be a capable educational manager' (Kitavi and van der Westhuizen 1997: 251–2). Similarly, headteachers in Ghana are often appointed without any form of preparatory training. 'The Ghana Education Service seems to be working on the assumption that a successful classroom teacher necessarily makes an effective school administrator' (Amezu-Kpeglo 1990: 5). The appointment of headteachers is largely based on a teacher's seniority in 'rank' and 'teaching experience'. Oduro (2003: 310) notes that 'commitment to the provision and maintenance of facilities, salaries and others were given priority over headteachers' professional development'.

Kitavi and van der Westhuizen (1997) make the wider point that:

The means by which most principals in developing countries are trained, selected, inducted and in-serviced are ill-suited to the development of effective and efficient school managers ... neither the old nor the new educational system [in Kenya] gives attention to either formal training or induction of beginning school principals. (p. 251)

This argument also applies in South Africa:

In many instances ... headteachers come to headship without having been prepared for their new role ... As a result, they often have to rely on ... experience and common sense ... However, such are the demands being made upon managers now, including headteachers, that acquiring expertise can no longer be left to common sense and character alone; management development support is needed. (Tsukudu and Taylor 1995: 108–9)

Subsequent research in the Gauteng province (Bush and Heystek 2006: 66) shows that two-thirds of principals 'have not progressed beyond their initial degree while almost one third are not graduates'. Similar findings arise from van der Westhuizen et al.'s (2004: 1) enquiry in the Mpumalanga province: 'Wide-ranging changes in the education system have rendered many serving school principals ineffective in the management of their schools. Many of these serving principals lack basic management training prior to and after their entry into headship'. Bush et al.'s (2006a) systematic literature review, for the Matthew Goniwe School of Leadership and Governance, concludes that 'most school principals have not received adequate specialist preparation for their leadership and management roles' (p. 13). This evidence has contributed to a recent government decision to introduce a new national qualification (Advanced Certificate in Education: School Leadership), which is being piloted in 2007–09 (Department of Education 2007). Subject to the findings of the evaluation, the ACE may become a mandatory qualification for new principals (Bush et al. 2007a).

A significant exception to the general position may be found in the Seychelles where the Ministry of Education, in partnership with the University of Warwick (UK), is providing training at master's level for up to 100 senior managers over a five-year period. This is a significant step for a small education system with only 33 schools (Bush 2005).

Quality of provision

Because preparation for new principals is limited, there is inevitably little literature on the nature and quality of provision. One exception is the work of Tekleselassie (2002: 59) in Ethiopia. He reports on a 'major focus on the professionalisation of educational management'. However, most principals attend only a limited (one month) in-service course on school management. Such short-term training 'has never been popular among principals ... short-term training has less impact and is less motivating to trainees since such training does not lead to certification and salary improvements' (ibid.). The limitations of the training are perceived to be:

- Irrelevant and repetitive curriculum
- Unresponsive and ill-prepared trainees
- Incompetence of trainers
- Lack of nexus between the training and the kind of profile the Ministry of Education seeks
- Short duration of training and thus undue strain on trainees' time. (Tekleselassie 2002: 60).

An additional weakness is that the training occurs after appointment, leaving new principals unprepared for their responsibilities. This is also the case in Ghana where the training is 'in service' and usually provided by international agencies for selected schools, mostly drawn from urban and semi-urban areas. These agencies, including the World Bank, UNESCO, the DfID, the United States Agency for International Development (USAID) and the Canadian International Development Agency (CIDA), often determine the number and category of schools to be involved. Oduro (2003: 309) notes that 'the training programmes cease once the project is accomplished because the Ghana Education Service complains of lack of money to sustain them'. All 30 participants in Oduro's (2003) study complain that the training was not organised at the right time and should have *preceded* their appointment as headteachers.

Herriot et al. (2002) report on the development of headteacher support groups in Kenya. Such groups emerged as part of an in-service training programme for primary schools (PRISM). These groups were seen as 'central to the sustainability of good management in schools' (ibid.: 514) and their main purposes are:

- A forum for sharing ideas
- The development of school materials
- Addressing and solving management problems
- Generating income
- Staff development and sensitisation for heads, committees, teachers and the community
- Improving the delivery of education and examination performance. (Herriot et al. 2002: 518)

These authors conclude that 'the networking that is beginning to develop has had a "rippling effect" across schools and clusters but there is a long way to go' (ibid) to ensure its continued success.

Rizvi (2008) argues that leaders in Pakistan would benefit from effective leadership development: this should go

beyond developing sound technical expertise to include understanding of how managerial styles encourage teachers' emotional commitment towards their work; how a clear vision for schools they lead is based on certain fundamental values and beliefs; how teachers are engaged in the activity of leadership both individually and collaboratively; and how power within a school organisation is devolved, distributed and shared.

There is more evidence about the quality of leadership and management development in South Africa. Bush and Heystek's (2006: 67) survey in the Gauteng province provides detailed perceptions from the 34 per cent of principals who have taken specialist honours or master's degrees in educational management. They give positive ratings to several aspects of their courses, notably 'management of teaching and learning', 'learner management' and 'human resource management'. They are less satisfied with 'the management of physical facilities' and 'management of finance'. This latter point is particularly significant as the post-Apartheid government has decentralised many responsibilities to the school level, including budgeting, fund-raising and fee-setting.

The majority of South African principals do not have specific qualifications in management and have limited opportunities for leadership development. Most attend short in-service events, lasting only a few days, organised by the provincial departments of education. McLennan's (2000: 305) assessment of training in the Gauteng province is that such workshops are 'often poorly organised and irrelevant'. Bush and Heystek (2006: 72) conclude that training should be extended and recommend that 'management development for principals should take place *before* appointment' (emphasis added).

Bush and Heystek (2006) advocate expansion of university provision but caution that knowledge-based programmes need to be modified to ensure that they are directly relevant to participants' schools. The Government's Task Team on Education Management (Department of Education 1996: 24) was critical of much university provision: 'Management development practices ... have tended to focus on the collection of qualifications and certificates with little attention being paid to actual ability to transfer this newly acquired knowledge to the institutions in which managers work'. Van der Westhuizen et al. (2004: 717) make a similar point in concluding their evaluation of management training in the Mpumalanga province:

> The design and content of training programmes should be geared towards developing requisite skills and knowledge to enable trainees to transfer their skills and knowledge ... to the school situation.

The new ACE: School Leadership programme, being piloted from 2007 to 2009, includes several elements designed to improve leadership and management practice, including mentoring, networking and site-based assessment (Bush et al. 2007b; Department of Education 2007).

Selection and induction

In the absence of formal requirements for leadership qualifications or training, administrators and/or communities require alternative criteria for recruiting and selecting principals. In developing countries, as we noted earlier, these are often related to the length of teaching experience, sometimes coupled with candidates' perceived competence as teachers. The criteria used in Africa are varied and unreliable. 'Kenya was no exception where many headteachers had been identified on the basis of dubious qualifications often of a personal nature rather than relevant experience and proven skills in the field of management' (Herriot et al. 2002: 510). These personal factors often include gender, and males dominate in Kenya with 93 per cent of primary school headteachers being male:

> A gender dimension in education management in Kenya is a subject that has not attracted many studies. It has been established nevertheless that women are not well represented in senior positions [including] headteachers. There are many factors which contribute to low represen-tation of women in key positions, not least patriarchy. (Herriot et al. 2002: 512)

Bush and Heystek's (2006) research in the Gauteng province of South Africa shows that 66 per cent of principals are male. Buckland and Thurlow (1996), referring to South Africa generally, say that 'serious ... gender distortions in the management cadre place ... women at a significant disadvantage'.

In Ghana, women are acutely under-represented in school headship, espe-cially in rural areas. This is largely attributable to the cultural context. Women are considered to be weak and are discouraged from taking up teaching posts in deprived areas. As a result, 'some girls felt that it wasn't worth studying hard or even coming to school because the female role models they encountered in the villages were either farmers, seamstresses or fishmongers and housewives who "give plenty birth"' (Oduro and MacBeath, 2003: 445).

These examples illustrate Gronn and Ribbins's (2003: 91) point that 'cultur-ally grounded recruitment and selection regimes generate particular occupa-tional profiles'. While this often leads to a male-dominated principalship, as in the examples above, the dominance of women in most professional settings in the Seychelles is reflected in the appointment of principals, with 27 of the 33 schools being led by females (Bush et al., in press).

Tekleselassie (2002) reports on a change in the 'placement' process for new principals in Ethiopia. Before 1994, 'the assignment of principals was largely conducted on the basis of the applicants' degree or diploma in educational administration' (p. 57). The new process involves teachers electing principals from among the teachers at the school. Initially, this is for two years and a re-election must be preceded by 'performance evaluation'. 'Colleagues, students, parents and the district office will assess the principal biannually to determine re-election for the second term. Then the district office must approve the election' (p. 59). Tekleselassie (2002: 59) concludes that 'elected school principals are the ones who are either outstanding in their teaching assignments, or those who are popular among colleagues or their superiors'. The process appears to include bureaucratic, democratic and political aspects leading to unpredictable outcomes.

Oduro (2003) identifies two main strategies that are employed by the Ghana Education Service in the appointment of headteachers. The first is *appointment through direct posting* which involves appointing newly trained teachers to lead schools, especially in the rural areas. The unattractiveness of rural life appears to have made working in rural schools non-competitive among teachers, who might otherwise have had aspirations to be appointed as headteachers. The second strategy is *appointment through selection interviews*, which is largely associated with the appointment of urban school headteachers. Candidates for interviews are selected through recommendation. The selection, according to the headteachers in Oduro's (2003) study, is largely influenced by a teacher's seniority in 'rank' and 'teaching experience'.

Harber and Davies (1997) say that headteachers in developing countries 'are chosen because they are good at one thing (teaching) and then put into the managerial role, which can demand quite different skills' (p. 77). Pheko (2008) notes that, in Botswana, '"good" teachers are appointed to school leadership without any qualifications or skills for school leadership and management'. Harber and Davies (1997: 67) add that heads also face 'frequent and compulsory' transfer which 'could happen at very awkward times, thereby creating extra workloads for those left behind'.

Oplatka (2004) points out that even teaching experience may not be necessary. 'In some African countries (e.g. Nigeria), principals are not even appointed on criteria of quality regarding their own performance in teaching. Many of them have never been in a classroom, since political connections may be a dominant factor in their appointment' (p. 434).

This is not the case in Ghana where Oduro (2003) notes that teaching experience, or acquisition of a professional qualification in teaching, is a necessary condition for one's appointment to leadership positions in basic and secondary schools. Even where political pressures influence the appointment of a headteacher, the appointee must necessarily be a trained teacher.

These examples illustrate the wider problem that principals in developing countries rarely have specific qualifications in educational leadership and management. They are expected to handle all the demands of leading schools in very difficult circumstances without any preparation for the role. In most countries, there is also no effective induction for new leaders.

Induction

There is only limited literature on the induction of principals in developing countries. This is almost certainly because there is little formal induction for leaders in such settings. As Kitavi and van der Westhuizen (1997: 260) put it, 'too often, and without consideration, principals in developing countries like Kenya are tossed into the job without pre-service training, without guarantee of in-service training, and without support from their employers'. They report that most experienced principals overcame their problems through trial and error. However, 'beginning principals in developing countries like Kenya need well-structured induction strategies that will make them effective and efficient educational managers. Without special attention to the entry year problems of beginning principals ... other attempts at improving the quality of education in developing countries may yield few results' (p. 260). This latter point is crucial; the quality of provision must be left to chance in the absence of effective leadership preparation and induction.

Kitavi and van der Westhuizen (1997: 261–2) advocate eight induction strategies for new principals:

1. Assign a veteran principal to assist the new appointee.
2. Provide manuals for new principals.
3. Ensure a smooth transition by involving the outgoing principal.
4. Orient the new principal to the school and its community.
5. Encourage networking with other principals.
6. Encourage principals to allow their deputies to 'shadow' them to gain experience.
7. Visits to other schools.
8. Provide courses in educational management.

Several of these ideas do not require significant expenditure but are likely to be helpful in supporting and developing new principals.

In Ghana, Oduro (2003) reports that it is common practice, especially in rural schools, for headteachers to be left unsupported after appointment. Most headteachers assume duty with little or no knowledge of their job descriptions. One comments that:

> I was appointed all of a sudden to be the head, which I wasn't expecting. I didn't know many things involved in it. For instance, I didn't know keeping financial records or preparing for auditing was part of the headteacher's job'. (Ibid.: 298).

The result is that headteachers tend to depend principally on trial and error approaches in carrying out their leadership tasks. Similar difficulties arise in Botswana, where heads 'feel ill equipped for the post' (Pheko 2008: 78). Induction may be available but this may be up to two years after taking up the post.

Inadequate, or no, induction compound the problems arising from a lack of pre-service preparation. Principals are appointed on the basis of their teaching qualifications and experience, and are then left to learn 'on the job'. When mistakes are being made, children's learning is likely to be affected.

The experience of new principals

It is evident from the discussion so far that, when new principals in developing countries take up their posts, they have not been adequately prepared for their responsibilities and cannot expect any meaningful induction. Tekleselassie (2002: 60) refers to the 'overload' affecting principals in Ethiopia.

Requiring principals to embark on such a demanding career without specific preparation is a recipe for personal stress and system failure, and also has serious ethical implications. As one participant in Pheko's (2008: 79) study of Botswana explains, I was 'thrown in the deep end without a life-line'.

Kitavi and van der Westhuizen (1997: 253) describe the world of novice principals 'as one filled with considerable anxiety, frustration and professional isolation … an increasingly clear picture shows new principals who cannot serve as instructional leaders, who tend to seek moral and ethical identities and suffer from feelings of stress associated with their new roles'.

These authors surveyed 100 new principals from all eight Kenyan provinces and achieved a 65 per cent response rate. One question related to the 'most serious problems facing beginning principals'. The main responses are shown in Table 7.1 and indicate that the problems facing new principals are primarily to do with practical issues related to students, parents, resources and staff. Only the issue of 'English as a medium of instruction' relates to the school's supposedly core function of teaching and learning. This suggests that the new leaders are preoccupied with these obstacles rather than focusing on their educational role. These issues are similar to those facing more experienced leaders but 'beginning principals seemed to experience them with greater intensity' (Kitavi and van der Westhuizen 1997: 260).

Table 7.1 Most serious problems facing beginning principals in Kenya

Rank	Item
1.	Students who cannot pay school fees
2.	Shortage of school equipment
3.	Students who cannot buy books
4.	Shortage of physical facilities
5.	Staff residential accommodation
6.	Installing telephones
7.	Parental illiteracy
8.	Students travelling long distances
9.	Lack of playground
10.	Use of English as a medium of instruction
11.	Clean water problem
12.	Locating suitable social club
13.	Inaccessibility of parents

Source: adapted from Kitavi and van der Westhuizen 2002: 255. This table was published in *International Journal of Educational Development*, 17(3), Kitavi, M. and van der Westhuizen, P., 'Problems facing beginning principals in developing countries: a study of beginning principals in Kenya', pp. 251–63, Copyright Elsevier (1997)

The expectations of principals in Ethiopia are similar to those indicated for Kenya. Tekleselassie (2002: 60–1) notes that 'the roles assigned to the principal portray the ones in bureaucratic and traditional organisations in which rules and procedure, rather than collaboration, teamwork and shared decision-making, govern action'. Despite this critical comment, the activities seem to provide for a more substantial instructional leadership role than that indicated in the Kenyan research.

Oduro (2003) explains that, in Ghana, the workload of primary headteachers depends on whether they are *attached* or *detached*. Attached headteachers are obliged to teach and handle all subjects on the school timetable alongside administrative and management tasks, while detached headteachers perform only administrative and management tasks. His study of 20 new headteachers in one Ghanaian district shows that all attached headteachers complained about a heavy workload. In rural areas, a shortage of teachers compelled some headteachers to handle more than one class. One notes that:

I have 231 pupils in my school with only four teachers. I'm handling Primary 3 and Primary 5. Quite recently, one of the teachers fell sick and I had to handle that class too. So one person handling three classes and doing administration at the same time ... how can I be effective? (Oduro 2003: 122–3)

The South African Task Team on Education Management (Department of Education 1996) stressed that management is important because it provides a supportive framework for teaching and learning:

Management in education is not an end in itself. Good management is an essential aspect of any education service, but its central goal is the promotion of effective teaching and learning ... The task of management at all levels is ultimately the creation and support of conditions under which teachers and their students are able to achieve learning ... The extent to which effective learning is achieved therefore becomes the criterion against which the quality of management is to be judged. (p. 27)

Despite this authoritative comment, which would be echoed in many other countries, there is only limited evidence of principals being developed for instructional leadership. Oplatka (2004: 434), for example, states that 'in most developing countries ... instructional leadership functions are relatively rare in schools, and principals are likely to adopt a stance in favour of administration and management'. Bush and Heystek's (2006) research in the Gauteng province of South Africa shows that most principals want training in finance and human resource management. Only 27.2 per cent of their respondents identify the management of teaching and learning as a development need. These authors conclude that 'principals are not conceptualising their role as "leaders of learning"' (p. 74).

Kogoe (1986) claims that headteachers in Togo 'need to adopt leadership roles by closer instructional leadership' but he adds that, while teachers expect leadership, 'heads may prefer to see themselves as just administrators'. The emphasis on educational leadership is also noted in the National Policy document for education in Botswana:

The heads as the *instructional leaders*, together with the deputy and senior teachers, should take major responsibility for in-service training of teachers within their schools, through regular observations of teachers and organisational workshops, to foster communication between teachers on professional matters and to address weaknesses. (Republic of Botswana 1994, in Pansiri, in press, emphasis added)

Such policy prescriptions are not always fulfilled in practice. Pansiri's (in press) research with 240 teachers shows that 70 per cent say that they receive constructive feedback on their teaching but 71 per cent add that senior management team (SMT) members do not give demonstration lessons or provide coaching on how to handle certain topics. He concludes that 'there is an urgent need for the Ministry of Education to develop an in-service module for SMTs and teachers on instructional leadership'.

In-service development

In developing countries, including many small island states, pre-service preparation is rare and the limited resources are devoted to in-service support (Bush et al., in press). Crossley and Holmes (1999: 24) stress the importance of providing support for leaders in remote island communities. They emphasise the value of exchanges, visits and attachments, information and networking, and technical meetings.

Cardno and Howse's (2004) review of secondary school principals in Fiji shows the breadth of development activities engaged in by their interviewees. These range from university degrees and diplomas to management workshops and various types of on-the-job support. Despite, or perhaps because of, this diversity, these principals complain that 'the nature of current training is ad hoc and the initiatives are not formalised' (ibid.: 24). Billot's (2003: 16) study of Tonga concludes that principals 'saw a need for skills and competencies that supported teaching and learning, with effective management skills being of less importance'.

Scott's (2001: 247) report of the Lakehead project in nine Eastern Caribbean nations sets out the intention 'to provide head teachers and senior education personnel with the skills and knowledge and the management and supervisory processes necessary for the effective running of the schools in the respective countries'. While they warn of the dangers of adopting Western paradigms, the structure and content of the modules, including management, leadership, resource planning, pastoral care and instruction, seem very similar to what Bush and Jackson (2002) describe as an international curriculum for school leadership development.

Bezzina (2001: 117) refers to the importance of lifelong learning for leaders and notes the particular value of in-service development for principals who were not 'adequately trained, prepared or exposed before taking up their posts'.

Conclusion: a new approach to school leadership in developing countries

The evidence presented in this chapter shows that school leaders in developing countries manage their schools in very difficult circumstances. These nations face severe economic, social, health and educational problems. Principals are usually appointed without specific preparation, receive little or no induction, have limited access to suitable in-service training and enjoy little support from the local or regional bureaucracy.

There are many reasons for this unsatisfactory situation. Most countries have very limited educational budgets and leadership preparation is seen as a low priority. Donor countries and international agencies have introduced training initiatives but these are rarely sustained beyond the initial funding period. While the need for principalship training is widely recognized (for example, Commonwealth Secretariat 1996), translating perceived need into effective provision has proved to be elusive (Bush and Oduro 2006).

Another problem is the lack of capacity among those responsible for appointing, training and supporting headteachers. Many of these officials are no better qualified than the principals. The long distances, and inadequate infrastructure, mean that principals in rural areas are rarely visited, increasing their sense of isolation. Shortages of teachers and material resources exacerbate this problem (Bush and Oduro 2006).

It would be easy, but unwise, to advocate improved processes based on models in Western countries. As Watson (2001: 29) demonstrates, 'educational policies cannot easily be transplanted from one national and social context to another'. Advocating specific forms of leadership development should be avoided unless they are based firmly on local needs and cultural imperatives (Bush et al., in press). What is more likely to succeed is a set of recommendations firmly grounded in the realities of schools in developing nations. Even then, such prescriptions can be translated into reality only through meaningful and long-term partnerships with governments, international agencies and universities in the developed world. The analysis and recommendations below are based on the assumption that funding would be provided to ensure effective implementation and long-term development.

Preparation

It is evident that preparation for school principals is inadequate in almost all developing countries. Most heads are appointed without any specific management training and few are able to access suitable in-service opportunities following appointment. While pre-service provision is highly desirable, this is inevitably more expensive because it is not always possible to identify those who are likely to be appointed as principals. Targeting the limited resources at newly appointed heads is much more cost-effective. This can also be seen as an important part of their induction (see below) (Bush and Oduro 2006).

The other advantage of in-service provision is that it can relate directly to the specific context facing the beginning principal. Crow (2001) distinguishes between professional and organisational socialisation. The former relates to preparation to enact the role of principal while the latter concerns adaptation to the particular school context. In-service preparation enables these two phases to be linked.

Development programmes in Western countries are often delivered by universities, governments or other agencies, are usually sustained over many months or years and typically lead to an academic or professional qualification. There are several problems in applying this approach to developing countries. The limited budgets available are unlikely to fund such a lavish model at an appropriate scale to meet the need. There is also limited capacity to develop, lead and facilitate such programmes. It would be sensible, therefore, to aim at more modest provision for the new principals accompanied by a 'train the trainers' course at a higher level. Linking the training to a qualification is likely to motivate participants (Tekleselassie 2002) and to raise the status of principals in their communities. As we noted earlier, an Advanced Certificate in Education: School Leadership, is being piloted in South Africa from 2007 to 2009.

Selection and induction

In the absence of a pre-service management qualification, the recruitment and appointment processes cannot be underpinned by formal prerequisites. Developing a clear job description, and linking candidates' experience to these requirements, provides a useful starting point. As more principals experience training, they may also be able to nominate suitable candidates based on job-related practice in their current schools. As we noted earlier, however, such rational processes are often undermined by political and cultural factors. One of these relates to gender and it is important that women have equal opportunities for promotion to senior posts, including headships.

The in-service training suggested above should make a valuable contribution to principals' induction. It also provides the potential for networking that could be sustained beyond the life of the course. Developing effective networks for both experienced and beginning principals may reduce their isolation.

Appropriate training, recruitment and selection do not ensure that principals are equipped with the requisite skills, attitudes, knowledge and motivation to lead their school effectively. Further support from their superordinates, and their local communities, are essential if their schools, and the students they serve, are to succeed and help their countries to compete in an increasingly challenging global economy.

8

The impact of leadership development

Introduction

In Chapter 3, we outlined the evidence that leadership development contributes to modified leadership and management practice, and to enhanced school and student outcomes. There is a widespread belief in the efficacy of development programmes, leading to the introduction and growth of such interventions in many countries (Hallinger 2003c; Huber 2004a; Watson 2003b). Governments are investing substantial sums in leadership development because they believe that it will produce better leaders and more effective schools' systems. Individuals are also contributing their time, and often their own resources, to their own professional development because they think that it will enhance their career prospects and make them better leaders. However, as we noted in Chapter 3, the empirical evidence for such assumptions is modest. In this chapter we address the intended impact of leadership development, consider models designed to assess such effects, and examine the evidence that preparation and development succeed in enhancing leadership practice and producing better educational institutions.

The purpose of leadership and management development

The impact of leadership preparation, induction and ongoing support cannot be assessed independently of the intended outcomes of such activities. An informed judgement about their effects depends on the nature and purpose of leadership development. There is limited discussion of this issue in the literature and those few sources tend to focus almost exclusively, and often uncritically, on student outcomes or the vaguer notion of 'school improvement'. The purpose of this section is to examine the aims of leadership development with a view to providing categories of 'impact' against which programmes and activities can be assessed. Huber (2004a: 97) argues that the aims of leadership development are themselves derived from wider educational goals. Clearer specification of such goals should help in designing appropriate leadership development activities.

In simple terms, the purpose of leadership development is to produce more effective leaders. An everyday definition of effectiveness is that the intended outcomes of an activity are achieved. Leadership programmes and activities need to be judged against this criterion. Do such processes produce better leaders and, critically, are certain approaches likely to be more successful than others in achieving such outcomes? These questions underpinned a review of 34 NCSL evaluations, undertaken by Bush et al. (2007b).

The main reported criteria for judging the effectiveness of educational leaders are:

- They produce beneficial effects on pupil learning, as measured by test scores (Heck 2003; Leithwood et al. 2006; Naylor et al. 2006).
- They produce beneficial effects on pupil attitudes and 'engagement' (Leithwood et al. 2006).
- They produce improvements in employee, and particularly teacher, motivation, capability and performance (Leithwood et al. 2006).
- They promote equity and diversity (Department of Education 1996; Lumby and Coleman 2007; McLennan and Thurlow 2003).
- They encourage democracy and participation (McLennan and Thurlow 2003).

These factors provide criteria for assessing the value and impact of leadership development programmes and activities. The challenges involved in designing, and evaluating, preparation and development initiatives may be expressed through a series of questions:

1. Is the main purpose of the activity to develop individual leaders or to promote wider leadership development? (Bush et al. 2007b; Hartley and Hinksman 2003; Watson 2003b)
2. Should leadership development be underpinned by succession planning, or be targeted at the needs and aspirations of individual leaders? (Bush et al. 2007b; NCSL 2006d, 2007)
3. Should leadership development be standards based, or promote a more holistic approach? (Brundrett et al. 2006; Male 2006; Reeves et al. 2001)
4. Should leadership development be content led or based around processes? (Walker and Carr-Stewart 2006)
5. Should leadership development programmes aim at inculcating a specific repertoire of leadership practices? (Leithwood et al. 2006)

6. Should leadership learning be predominantly campus based or field based? (Heck 2003)
7. Should leadership learning address issues of equity and diversity? (Bush et al. 2006c, 2007b; Lumby and Coleman 2007)

Developing leaders or leadership development?

Bush et al.'s (2007b) meta analysis of NCSL evaluation reports, linked to a review of the leadership development and adult learning literature, shows that, while the term 'leadership development' is widely used, most NCSL programmes are targeted at individuals and may more accurately be regarded as 'leader development'. They conclude that the wider issue of leadership development for school improvement needs more attention. This argument applies to leadership preparation in many countries and connects to the traditional model of 'singular' leadership rather than the currently fashionable 'distributed leadership' (Harris 2004).

Hartley and Hinksman (2003) say that leadership development requires a focus on structure and systems as well as people and social relations. Tusting and Barton (2006) argue that there is a movement away from the individual towards the emergent and collective as well as providing greater recognition of the significance of the context for leadership learning. Given the popularity of interactive learning, such as networking, a stronger focus on school-wide leadership development appears to be timely (Bush et al. 2007b).

The continuing emphasis on developing individual leaders arises partly because leadership is often equated with *headship*. Much writing ostensibly about leadership and/or management development is actually concerned solely (for example, Watson 2003b) or primarily (for example, Huber 2004a) with preparing or training principals. The only statutory programme among the many offerings from the NCSL is for aspiring heads, the NPQH. The new ACE: School Leadership programme in South Africa is also targeted at principals. In North America, the lens widens somewhat to include assistant principals but it is still concerned with individual senior leaders. This focus is reflected in the nature and content of development activities and in the evaluation processes used to assess the quality and impact of such programmes. Genuine and sustained school improvement is only likely to occur if the thrust shifts from preparing individuals to empowering and developing schools as organisations. As the South African Task Team on Education Management asserts, there should be 'a shift in emphasis from "training" the individual towards support for individual development within the context of organisational development' (Department for Education 1996: 33).

Succession planning or meeting individual needs

Watson (2003b: 9) asks a key question: 'to what extent does any training or other development system draw upon an individualised understanding of the developmental needs, and the particular strengths and weaknesses, of the particular headteacher?' This point connects to the key issue of whether programmes should be standardised or personalised. The NCSL's new model NPQH stresses personalisation but it also links development to the national standards for headship (see below). While it can be argued that any qualification needs an element of consistency, to ensure high-quality graduates and equality of treatment for all applicants, personalisation is necessary to take account of aspirants' diverse pre-course experience and the different circumstances likely to be encountered by heads working in different contexts.

A personalised approach may succeed in meeting the aspirations of individual leaders, but is unlikely to ensure that national and community needs are met. A major national responsibility for any society is to ensure a sufficient supply of leaders to meet the perceived demand. As the NCSL (2006c: 5) points out, succession planning provides a 'systematic approach to leadership recruitment and development', in contrast to 'the ad hoc approach' that is the likely outcome of a process that is driven wholly by individual needs. Succession planning is regarded as essential 'to ensure there is a supply and flow of high quality candidates for headship and leadership teams' (NCSL 2007: 16). When a mandatory qualification is introduced, as in England for example, this constitutes an additional 'hurdle' for potential heads that may restrict supply in the short-term, or act as a disincentive in the longer term.

Standards-based or holistic development

The development and use of 'standards' is gaining ground in the preparation of school leaders, notably in Australia, England, New Zealand, Scotland, South Africa and the USA, prompting Male (2006: 58) to comment that 'the adoption of standards for school leaders is well on the way to becoming a global phenomenon'. Brundrett et al. (2006: 101) add that 'standards-based programmes have assumed apparent dominance in the training and development of school leaders in both England and New Zealand'.

The focus on standards may be understood as part of an ongoing fascination with the technical aspects of school management and leadership. The argument appears to be that, by articulating a clear set of expectations for leaders, the standards provide a basis for measuring performance, during and after training, and that successful completion of such standards-based programmes provides at least baseline competence in the leadership role. Reeves (2004: 43) asserts that 'one of the hallmarks of effective leadership evaluation is that it is standards based'. The Scottish Qualification for Headship (SQH), for example, is based on the Standard for Headship in Scotland which:

> sets out the key aspects of professionalism and expertise which the Scottish education system requires of those who are entrusted with the leadership and management of its schools. (SOEID 1998, in Reeves et al. 2001: 38)

The danger of a standards-based approach is that it may atomise and over-simplify the complex role of the principal. Specifying a set of specific competences assumes that they are generally applicable across all contexts. There are also difficulties in assessing whether potential heads have reached an appropriate standard (Male 2006: 64). This presents another challenge in that measurable outcomes are likely to be privileged over those that may be just as important but are less easily assessed. Brundrett et al. (2006: 100) warn that such competency frameworks lead to 'one size fits all' models that are inappropriate for the complexity of school leadership in the twenty-first century.

Content-led or process-rich programmes

Bush et al. (2007b) point to the importance of school leaders being co-constructors of their learning, because they are usually well-educated senior professionals with a highly developed sense of their own learning needs. Their meta-analysis of NCSL evaluations shows that participants mostly prefer process-rich learning and reject 'content-heavy' programmes. The most valued activities are networking, through face-to-face events or purposeful school visits. Linked to the latter, learning is enhanced where schools are the main foci of learning, enabling participants to engage with real, and often pressing, problems rather than artificial or simulated cases. They add that this twenty-first-century model offers a much more flexible approach, linked to the personal, and often emergent, needs of learners, with a strong element of school-based learning and a clear recognition that senior professionals are entitled to participate in constructing their own learning agenda. Walker and Carr-Stewart (2006: 32) add that new principals need opportunities to reflect on what has been successful in their own practice. However, it may be argued that provider-led learning also has merit. It provides a consistent approach, it enables the dissemination of good practice derived from theory and research, and it draws on the expertise of more experienced leaders as well as academics.

A specific repertoire of leadership practices or a contingency approach?

Leithwood et al.'s (2006: 6) 'seven strong claims about school leadership' include the comment that 'almost all successful leaders draw on the same repertoire of basic leadership practices'. While acknowledging the importance of context, they assert that this is significant for the application of this repertoire, rather than requiring a different skills set. The four basic practices are:

- Building vision and setting directions
- Understanding and developing people
- Redesigning the organisation
- Managing the teaching and learning programme.
  (Ibid.)

These categories are quite broad but, in principle, they provide a framework for the design, and evaluation, of leadership development programmes. However, we have already noted a growing trend to personalise programmes in response to individual needs and contextual variables. When Bush and Heystek (2006) asked South African principals about their development needs, the 'management of finance' was the most often stated requirement. This is because of the post-Apartheid shift to self-managing schools, which has imposed several new budgeting and fee-setting responsibilities on school governing bodies and principals. A development framework that excluded this dimension would not meet the needs of South African principals.

Campus-based or field-based learning?

Most preparation programmes, notably those operated by universities, tend to be campus based. Participants work through a set curriculum and are assessed on their understanding, and sometimes their application, of certain principles of leadership and management. However, there is a growing view that leadership learning should be field based, taking place in schools not in providers' classrooms. 'The school administrator's role is best learned in the field by doing and under the guidance of experienced, exemplary mentor principals' (Heck 2003: 252).

Bush et al.'s (2007b) meta-analysis of NCSL evaluations provides evidence that participants prefer to use their own school for learning, inspired by the notion of making 'the workplace the workshop'. They argue that workplace learning may be accelerated:

- By carrying out school-based enquiries
- By engaging in school visits, particularly where they are tightly focused
- Where school change is inspired by skilfully planned external 'interventions'
- Where several school leaders are engaged in leadership learning at the same time.
(Ibid.: 83–4)

However, Bush et al. (2007b: 84) also note the value of off-site activity: 'Participants on several programmes appear to value such sessions because of their potential for networking but they also seem to provide space for reflection.' The new South African ACE: School Leadership programme adopts a blended learning approach. Campus-based learning is supported by school-based mentoring, networking, and site-based assessment (Bush et al. 2007a).

Leadership for equity and diversity

In many parts of the world, women are under-represented in educational leadership and management, even though they generally form a majority of the teaching force. Such discrimination has been reported in Australia (Blackmore 2006), China (Coleman et al. 1998), England (Coleman 2002), Greece (Kaparou and Bush 2007), South Africa (Buckland and Thurlow 1998; Bush et al. 2006a) and the USA (Shakeshaft 1989). Black and minority ethnic (BME) leaders are also marginalised in many countries, including England and the USA (Bush et al. 2006c, 2007). In South Africa, the majority black African population still experiences discomfort and discrimination when seeking and holding leadership posts in the former white, Indian and 'coloured' schools (Bush and Moloi 2007).

These problems provide a challenge for those responsible for leadership development programmes. There are two key questions that need to be addressed:

- How, if at all, should the recruitment to, and the design, delivery and assessment of, such activities reflect a focus on equity and diversity? Bush et al. (2007) argue that an undifferentiated model inevitably means an approach tailored to the needs of the majority white population.
- Should the design and content of leadership programmes differ for minority groups? Lumby and Coleman (2007: 63) comment that training for BME leaders should not re-create them as 'clones of their white colleagues'.

Resolving such questions is not straightforward, and there are differing views among BME leaders (Bush et al. 2007), but they need to be at the heart of design and delivery processes and not thrust to the margin. Commenting on the 'new model' NPQH, the NCSL (2007: 3) states that 'NCSL aims to ensure that those recruited as trainee headteachers are representative of the diverse workforce and school population'. While this is welcome, equal attention needs to be given to content and delivery if such programmes are to be suitable for minority candidates.

Evaluation and impact models

The purpose of this section is to examine impact models to assess their salience for leadership development. There is ample evidence that programmes are subject to evaluation but the approaches often employed are subject to two main limitations:

1. They rely mainly or exclusively on *self-reported evidence*. Participants are asked about their experience of the activity and, more rarely, about its impact on their schools. This is a weak approach because it is not subject to corroboration, for example by colleagues, and because it is inevitably subjective.
2. The evaluation is usually *short term*. Participants' views are often sought during and/or at the end of the development activity. It is widely recognised that the impact of interventions, such as a leadership programme, takes time. It is unlikely that significant changes in leadership practice will have occurred during the training period.

Even where these two pitfalls are avoided, there is still the problem of attributing beneficial effects to the development activity when there are likely to be many other contemporaneous events that could also contribute to change. However, addressing these two limitations would produce more credible, if not totally reliable, findings.

Huber (2004a: 92) sets out four questions designed to establish whether programmes 'meet expectations':

- Do they reach the goals established by their providers?
- Do they meet state requirements?
- Do they meet the expectations of the participating school leaders and the profession as a whole?
- Do they meet the expectations of the wider community?
  (Adapted from Huber 2004a: 92)

In assessing responses to his international enquiry, Huber (2004a: 93) concludes that evaluation data mainly relate to:

> The level of satisfaction achieved as requested from the participants ...
> There are hardly any follow-up assessments or external evaluations ... we
> know little about what is achieved by the programs and [their] relation-
> ship to program effectiveness because such studies were rarely conducted.

There have been three evaluations of the Scottish Qualification for Headship.
These mainly focus on candidates' self-reporting (see above) but there is also an
element of triangulation as the evaluation model also included insights from
candidates' mentors (Reeves et al. 2001).

Reeves (2004) advocates adopting Multidimensional Leadership Assessment
(MLA) to improve leadership evaluation. He comments that most current evaluation systems 'are ill equipped to help them achieve their potential' (p. 97).
His model involves 10 dimensions of leadership and requires the specification
of performance levels. This matrix approach, specifying what should be measured, and the extent to which each dimension has been achieved, provides a
useful basis for evaluating leadership development.

In England, there is increasing concern about whether and how leadership
impacts on school outcomes. The official 'End to End Review' of School Leadership (DfES 2004b) demonstrates the government's keen interest in exploring
this issue:

> Greater understanding is needed of the linkages and mediators between
> leadership and educational attainment and social outcomes ... [there is a]
> lack of consensus about the contribution of different elements to the link-
> ages, indirect effects and mediating factors for improving school leader-
> ship. (Para. 22)

The Department for Education and Skills (DfES) also commissioned a paper 'to
assist them to think about how to evaluate the impact of leadership on school
outcomes' (Leithwood and Levin 2004: 2). These authors begin by noting that
'linking leadership to student outcomes in a direct way is very difficult to do'
(p. 2). They propose a six-stage model linking leadership preparation to
student outcomes (see Figure 8.1). Despite their comment that research should
'measure an expanded set of outcome variables ... beyond just short-term
pupil learning' (p. 4), the final stage of the model is 'improved student
outcomes'.

Leithwood and Levin (2004: 5) say that Figure 8.1 'captures the range of
possible expectations for theoretically framing the evaluation of leadership
programmes as well as leadership itself'.

Leithwood and Levin (2004: 25) conclude that 'a study that seeks to assess
the impact that school leadership can have on school outcomes faces some
formidable challenges'. However, their model does provide a possible basis for

Leadership preparation experiences

⬇

Qualities of effective programmes   Participant satisfaction

⬇

Changes in knowledge, disposition and skills

⬇

Changes in leadership practices in schools

⬇

Participation satisfaction   Altered classroom conditions

⬇

Improved student outcomes

Figure 8.1 Framework for the evaluation of leadership programmes
(*Source:* adapted from Leithwood and Levin 2004.)

evaluating the impact of school leadership development on school and student outcomes.

Bush et al. (2006b) adapt this model to interpret the findings from their evaluation of the impact of NCSL's New Visions programme. They were seeking to assess the extent to which programme learning can be transferred to the participant's school. Their research went beyond self-reporting to gauge the in-school effects of the programme, from four contrasting perspectives:

- The participating headteacher
- A leadership team member
- A classroom teacher
- The governing body chair.

Bush et al.'s (2005) evaluation of the impact of NCSL team programmes involved 10 case studies sampled purposively on the basis that either the evaluation team, or the respective programme teams, regarded them as being likely to demonstrate evidence of impact. Within each school, the researcher conducted individual or focus group interviews, with a range of participants and stakeholders, including the NCSL's facilitators, and analysed relevant school documents. The data were interpreted using the Leithwood and Levin (2004) impact model. This model is also being used in the evaluation of the South African ACE: School Leadership pilot programme (Bush et al. 2007a).

Heck's (2003) approach to evaluation involved survey research with 150 beginning assistant principals and their supervising principals. Principals rated the quality of their assistant's performance of 21 tasks in three categories:

- School governance
- School culture
- School instruction.

These data were linked to the findings of a separate questionnaire designed to gather information about assistant principals' professional and organisational socialisation. Although this approach goes beyond self-reporting, Heck (2003: 243) adds a caution that 'no single evaluation model is likely to capture the entire richness of the school administrator's role'.

In the next section, we examine the findings from these impact studies.

Evaluating the impact of leadership development

Self-reported data

As noted earlier, many evaluations of leadership development activities tend to rely wholly or mainly on self-reported data. One such example is the initial study of the impact of the NCSL programme, 'Leading from the Middle' (LftM) (Naylor et al. 2006). These authors received 710 replies from a population of 1030 middle leaders, a response rate of 68.9 per cent, to a series of questions about the impact of LftM. The statements were:

- I am confident as a leader.
- My team is led effectively.
- My team has a clear impact on pupil progress.

Responses to these statements referred to their pre-LftM perceptions and their feelings after completing the course, although the data were collected only following the programme. The responses show a significant increase in confidence levels after the course. Participants also claimed that the impact of their teams, and the teams' effects on pupil progress, had increased considerably although less than their improvement in confidence.

The authors acknowledge that these findings may represent 'post-programme euphoria' and also note the limitations of such self-reported data. However, they conclude by asserting that 'the LftM programme has had a significant short-term impact on those surveyed' (ibid.: 14).

A similar approach has been used in three small-scale evaluations of the SQH (Reeves et al. 2001). Candidates were interviewed and their work was examined to see if there were any changes in their conceptions of school leadership and management. The majority of candidates felt that they have become more reflective and evaluative as a result of their experience of the programme. They also claimed 'a noticeable impact on candidates and their schools' (ibid.: 46). While this is self-reported data, the authors also note that 77 per cent of candidates' headteacher mentors agreed that candidates' practice had improved and that there were benefits for their schools.

Heck's (2003) study of 150 assistant principals, and their supervising principals, goes beyond self-reporting to include the perspectives of their superordinates. He notes that those candidates who had progressed to the principalship 'had developed a clear understanding of their role and responsibilities' (p. 247). Many attributed this to their internship and to the support provided by mentors. These new principals had also established strong support networks that sustained them during difficult periods.

Subjective judgements

Even less satisfactory than self-reported data are judgements based on subjective criteria. In several European countries, principals are subject to an evaluation process. This often seems to be highly unreliable. In Belarus, 'assessment is very subjective and vulnerable to the preferences of individuals making the evaluative decisions' (Zagoumennov and Shalkovich 2003: 19). Similarly, Pashiardis (2003: 39), referring to Cyprus, notes that there are 'no evaluative criteria specifically on the leadership or managerial roles of the principal'.

Role set analysis

The weaknesses of self-reporting can be addressed through adopting role set analysis. The perceptions of programme participants can be triangulated (Bush 2002) by seeking views from close colleagues at the school or workplace. This enables candidates' claims to be corroborated or challenged by the perceptions of those who should be aware of changes in practice. The present author adopted this approach in three impact studies, two for the NCSL and one in South Africa. In each case, interpretation of the data was undertaken using the Leithwood and Levin (2004) model (see above).

Bush et al. (2006b) examined the impact of the NCSL's 'New Visions' programme on school outcomes as part of a wider evaluation of this programme for new first-time headteachers. The research team observed group sessions and interviewed candidates about their experience of the programme. In particular, they also sought to address two impact-related evaluation objectives:

- To examine the impact of the programme upon participants and their schools.
- To consider the extent to which programme learning can be transferred to the participant's school.
(Ibid.: 192)

The research included case study work in a purposive sample of 15 schools in three regions. Researchers interviewed four people in each school to achieve respondent triangulation, and to gauge school effects from four contrasting perspectives:

- The *participant headteachers*, to examine which school developments they attributed to their New Visions experience
- *Leadership team members*, to assess whether there had been any changes in leadership practice, and classroom practice, arising from the programme
- *Classroom teachers*, to assess whether there had been any changes in classroom practice arising from the programme
- *Governing body chairs*, to establish whether there had been any impact on governing body practice, and wider aspects of school life, arising from the programme.
(Ibid.: 192).

The findings are structured according to the Leithwood and Levin (2004) model.

Participant satisfaction

The survey data (Bush and Glover 2005) showed satisfaction levels above 80 per cent and this was confirmed by case study data. This provides an important starting point for behavioural changes.

Changes in knowledge, disposition and skills

Many participants claimed significant gains in their confidence and personal development. These changes were often confirmed by role set members who noted participants' enthusiasm on their return from New Visions activities.

Changes in leadership practices

Participants and their role sets noted three main changes in leadership practice:

- A greater emphasis on shared leadership
- An enhanced focus on leadership for learning
- Specific changes in school organisation.

Altered classroom conditions

The enhanced focus on leadership for learning appears to have impacted on classroom practice in several ways:

- Higher expectations of staff
- Heads modelling good classroom practice
- Greater emphasis on monitoring classroom teaching and pupils' performance.

Improved student outcomes

The effects of the New Visions programme are filtered through many levels before they impact on this dimension but the authors noted two types of impact:

1. A determination to act on this issue, noted by role set members.
2. Some modest evidence of improvements, including removal from the 'serious weaknesses' category following Ofsted inspections, and improved examination and test results.
   (Bush et al. 2006b)

While this research produced significant evidence of impact arising from the New Visions experience, the authors note the 'diminishing influence' of the programme as the model moves through each phase. They also recommend a longer-term evaluation 'because leadership effects are likely to take time to impact on student outcomes' (ibid.: 197).

  Given the dominance of *leader* development, noted above, Bush et al.'s (2005) evaluation of the impact of two NCSL team programmes, *Developing Capacity for Sustained Improvement* (DCSI) and *Working Together for Success* (WTfS), provides a rare opportunity to assess the wider impact of leadership development initiatives targeted at a group of leaders. The evaluation involved 10 case studies of schools (five DCSI and five WTfS), which have completed, or embarked upon, one of these programmes. They were sampled purposively on the basis that either the evaluation team, or the respective programme teams, regarded them as being likely to demonstrate evidence of impact. Within each school, the researcher conducted individual or focus group interviews with a range of participants and stakeholders, and analysed relevant school documents. In addition, telephone interviews were held with NCSL facilitators.

The main findings from the WTfS schools were:

- Staff at all schools perceived a significant impact on the Senior Leadership Team (SLT), including greater clarity of individual SLT roles and enhanced team work.
- Most schools also developed teamworking beyond the SLT, including middle leaders, classroom teachers and governors.
- WTfS techniques were used extensively within all five schools.
- WTfS appears to have influenced the strategic planning process at some of the schools, notably in the use of WTfS techniques.
- The sustainability of the WTfS impact depends heavily on SLT stability. Senior staff departures are likely to weaken its impact.

The main findings from the DCSI schools were:

- Most schools seem to have enhanced SLT effectiveness but there are mixed views about the impact of DCSI. Some say that the programme acted as a catalyst while others suggest that progress was independent of DCSI.
- There was little evidence of any impact from DCSI techniques.
- Development planning appears to be more consultative in most schools and this was attributed to DCSI at two of them.
- The overall impact of DCSI is beneficial but limited.

The authors conclude that the five WTfS case study schools all show evidence of a significant impact from the programme. The techniques have become widely embedded in school practice and are used with staff, pupils and governors as well as within the leadership team. Changes in SLT practice are less widespread but WTfS has had an impact in some of the schools. The evidence from the DCSI schools was less compelling. While the participants enjoyed the sessions, none of them completed the intended programme and the lack of in-school activity means that it scarcely penetrated beyond the initial participants. This programme's impact has been modest (Bush et al. 2005).

Bush et al. (2007a) are conducting an evaluation of South Africa's pilot ACE: School Leadership programme, funded by the Zenex Foundation. The research will provide a comprehensive evaluation of the national field test programme in order to inform the development of the course and to provide advice to the Minister of Education. The evaluation is longitudinal with four phases:

1. *Preliminary work*, including a desk study of approaches to leadership development in other countries, and documentary analysis of course materials.
2. A *baseline study* of students to establish their motivation for taking part in the ACE, their previous qualifications and experience, and their attitudes to their leadership and management roles.
3. A *mid-term evaluation* to establish the experience of students during the programme.
4. An *impact study* to assess the nature and extent of effects from the ACE programme, including individual and school-level impact.

The research is unusual in planning an impact study from the outset, and linking it to earlier phases of the evaluation. The findings of the impact study will be compared with the baseline data to assess changes in leadership practice, classroom practice, and school and student outcomes, and interpreted using the Leithwood and Levin (2004) model. The findings will lead to informed advice to the Minister of Education about the viability and validity of the ACE programme as preparation for aspiring school principals.

Quantitative research

Leithwood et al. (2006) report on the evidence of leadership effects emerging from quantitative studies. They cite Hallinger and Heck's (1998) finding that leadership accounts for up to 7 per cent of the difference in pupil learning and achievement in schools. This figure rises to an astonishing 27 per cent when the combined impact of all sources of leadership is included, giving powerful support to the notion of distributed leadership (Leithwood et al. 2006: 12). These findings are not connected directly to leadership development but the clear implication is that systematic and effective preparation for leaders has the potential to impact in a significant way on school and learner outcomes.

Overview

The global interest in leadership development is predicated on the widespread assumption that it will lead to school improvement, and enhanced learning outcomes. The empirical evidence for this perspective is limited but the issue is increasingly being given attention, notably by the British government and the English NCSL. Assessing impact is difficult because of several conceptual and methodological problems. First, as we have seen, the purposes of education, and of educational leadership, are wide and varied. The efficacy of leadership activities needs to be tested against all these criteria if a comprehensive assessment of impact is to be made. In practice, however, impact studies tend to focus on the measurable outcomes sought by governments, notably student test scores. Secondly, even where improvements occur, it is very difficult to attribute them with confidence to a specific intervention, such as a leadership development programme, when there are many other contemporaneous changes. Thirdly, while leadership is widely regarded as the second most important factor affecting student outcomes, after classroom teaching, it is a mediated variable with leaders exercising their influence indirectly. This makes it difficult to assess the nature and extent of leaders' impact.

There are few studies of the impact of leadership development activities and they are often of limited validity, typically because they rely on short-term and self-reported findings. Role-set analysis serves to address the second of these problems but well planned and executed long-term studies are essential if the effects of leadership development are to be assessed with confidence. Leadership development is expanding as governments and individual leaders increasingly acknowledge its importance. The next step is to ensure that this public and private investment is subject to thorough and extended evaluation. Well-grounded evidence on the impact of leadership, and of leadership development, is a major research need.

9

The future of leadership development

Introduction: leadership matters

There is great, and widespread, interest in educational leadership and management, a trend that has been accelerating in the twenty-first century. The widely accepted belief that effective leadership is vital for successful schooling is increasingly being supported by evidence of its beneficial effects (Hallinger 2003a; Leithwood et al. 2006). Leadership is now recognised to be the second most significant factor influencing school and pupil outcomes, after classroom practice (Leithwood et al. 2006). Schools and colleges often succeed because of the skill and commitment of their principals and senior teams. Where there is failure, inadequate leadership is often a major contributory factor. As a result, 'school leadership has recently become one of the central concerns of educational policy makers' (Hallinger 2003b: 273).

Given the importance of educational leadership, the development of effective leaders should not be left to chance. It should be a deliberate process designed to produce the best possible leadership for schools and colleges. As the NCSL (2007: 17) succinctly argues, 'leadership must grow by design not by default'. Van der Westhuizen and van Vuuren (2007: 431) refer to the 'professionalisation' of the principalship, an explicit recognition that school leadership is a different role from teaching and requires separate and specialised preparation. 'Principalship in South Africa is on its way to becoming a fully-fledged profession with a unique career path' (ibid.). This is clearly true of many other countries, including England, Singapore and the USA, although van der Westhuizen and van Vuuren overstate the case when they claim that 'South Africa is one of the few countries that do not require a compulsory and specific qualification for principalship' (ibid.).

The trend towards systematic preparation and development of school and college leaders, while by no means universal, has advanced to the point where the argument is widely accepted. However, there is continuing and ongoing debate about the nature of such provision.

Content or process?

In Chapter 4, we drew on insights from nine countries to derive an international 'core' curriculum comprising five main themes:

- Instructional leadership
- Law
- Finance
- Managing people
- Administration.

The NCSL (2007: 6) draws on the work of Leithwood et al. (2006) to provide an alternative way of conceptualising the role of school leaders and, by implication, the 'curriculum' for school leadership development. It refers to 'a core set of leadership practices that form the "basics" of successful leadership'. These are:

- Building vision and setting directions
- Understanding and developing people
- Redesigning the organisation
- Managing the teaching and learning programme.

If these are the main practices of successful leaders, then development activities ought to be linked to the acquisition and refinement of the skills required to carry out such tasks effectively. While two items in the NCSL list match those in the international 'core curriculum', the others seem to require a different skills set. How do you develop leaders to build vision and redesign the organisation? Arguably, such practices require a greater emphasis on process than content.

As we noted in Chapter 4, there is extensive material on the use of different techniques in leadership development. The challenge is to find an appropriate mix of these approaches to meet the needs of leaders at different career stages, and in different contexts. The requirements of school principals in Africa, for example, are different to those of middle managers in developed countries, and preparation and support must be tailored to these individual and societal needs. Four central questions need to be addressed and resolved in ways that fit the specific educational context.

Where does leadership learning take place?

Bush et al. (2007b) say that the most successful learning experiences occur when there is a bridge between the work situation and the learning situation.

The NCSL (2007: 17) claims that 'a large amount of ... leadership learning should take place in school', but they also acknowledge that such work-based learning can be 'narrow and conservative' (ibid.: 18). Bush et al. (2007b) add that learning may be enhanced within the work situation, and through reflection, away from the normal context. There is no 'off-the-peg' solution to such dilemmas and course designers need to find a judicious and appropriate balance for their specific client group(s). As the NCSL (2007: 18) argues, 'a new alliance between learning on-the-job and off-site development' is required. The new South Africa ACE: School Leadership, for example, blends classroom learning with site-based mentoring and assessment, and district-wide networking (Bush et al. 2007a; Department of Education 2007).

Individual or group learning?

The most successful adult learning appears to grow from the identification of personalised learning needs. However, individualised learning is difficult to organise and can be expensive to deliver. For 'statutory provision', in particular, it also compromises the standardisation required to justify the 'national programme' label. The new version of the English NPQH, to be piloted from 2008, stresses personalised learning and it will be a challenge for programme leaders to facilitate this individual approach while still ensuring that new headteachers have reached an appropriate 'threshold' to be awarded the qualification.

Who leads development?

Huber (2004c: 98) argues that 'special consideration' needs to be given to the recruitment of those who are to lead development activities. Bush et al. (2007b) caution that people designated as tutors, mentors, coaches and facilitators may not understand their role and may have been selected on the basis that they are perceived to be, or to have been, successful leaders. Crow (2004: 304) expresses reservations about the use of 'veteran' principals for leadership preparation, a popular method in North America, because it is unlikely to promote creativity and innovation. The main alternative model is to employ university staff but they may lack credibility if they do not have school leadership experience. A central research question in the evaluation of the South African ACE: School Leadership programme is whether such academics will be able to adapt to the requirements of a practice-based course (Bush et al. 2007a). Crow (2004: 304) argues that the use of theory and research may offset the 'conservative orientation' of development led by experienced principals.

What are the most effective leadership learning processes?

School leaders are senior professionals who have a well-developed sense of their own learning needs. These are inevitably individual, so generalisation about the effectiveness of particular approaches is dangerous. However, Bush et al.'s (2007b) meta-analysis of NCSL evaluations provides an evidence-based overview of the value of the various processes used in its many development programmes.

Networking is the most favoured mode of leadership learning for NCSL participants (Bush et al. 2007b). It is 'live learning' and provides strong potential for ideas transfer. It is likely to be most effective when the networks have a clear purpose and are not simply opportunities for anecdotalism. Such peer learning may be an alternative, or a supplement, to activities led by tutors, who may carry alternative labels such as mentor, coach, trainer or *facilitator*. The key aspect of the latter role is that the relationship is essentially learner led, with the facilitator responding to the expressed needs of participants. Bush et al. (2007b) note that this is one of the widely applauded dimensions of NCSL programmes. Regardless of the label applied to the 'facilitator' role, the main variables in determining the success of such professional relationships are the training and prior experience of the facilitator, the matching process, and their ability to provide an appropriate and individualised balance of challenge and support.

Leadership and values

Leadership is strongly associated with the concept of values (Bush 2003; Bush and Glover 2003; Ng 2001). The NCSL (2007: 7) says that 'values are inextricably tied up with leadership … Values provide a moral compass and an anchor for the work of school leaders'. The assumption underpinning this view is that leaders have their own values that inform their decisions. A contrary opinion is that principals are simply expected to internalise the national policy agenda and implement it in their schools. Gunter (in press), for example, argues that the British government wanted a head-teacher who understood and could deliver the New Labour agenda.

This debate has clear implications for the nature of leadership development. Thody et al.'s (2007) review of school leadership preparation in Europe shows that those countries with highly centralised systems, such as Cyprus and Greece, were less likely to give a high priority to development of principals. Where training is provided, it is 'deeply legislative' (p. 46) rather than having a leadership orientation. In Cyprus, for example, in-service training for principals concerns 'management duties and responsibilities which the Ministry of

working well (Bush and Chew 1999). It is also consistent with the country's wider approach to public services and, therefore, suitable for the national context.

England has also adopted a singular national model of leadership preparation for potential headteachers. From 2009, it will be mandatory for new heads to possess the NPQH, designed by the NCSL for the government. Unlike Singapore, heads in England are appointed by school governing bodies, not by the state. However, they will not have the discretion to appoint an uncertified applicant, even one holding a university master's degree in educational leadership. As Gunter (in press) suggests, 'postgraduate programmes became sidelined in favour of national training programmes'. This 'single national focus' carries certain risks. Despite the intention to allow, even encourage, personalised [de]velopment, the outcome will be a headteacher accredited by the state against [a se]t of national standards. Given the mixed views of current NPQH graduates [(Bus]h et al. 2007), a lack of pluralism may mean that new heads receive only a [narro]w prescribed preparation for the challenges of school leadership (Bush

[The] USA provides the most obvious example of pluralism in leadership [preparat]ion. Responsibility for education rests with the 50 states and most of [req]uire principals to hold a recognised master's degree in educational [administra]tion. More than 500 universities provide leadership courses (Huber [...]). Only 76 of these are members of the prestigious University [Council for] Educational Administration, regarded by Huber (2004c: 276) as 'the [au]thority for qualification programs in the training of educational [leaders...]'varied landscape' (ibid.: 277) for school leadership preparation [...esse]ntial choice for potential school principals but most states pro[vide ...o]f consistency by requiring providers to adhere to the Interstate [School Leaders] Licensure Consortium (ISLLC) standards (Bjork and Murphy

[...ISL]LC standards not only aligned professional preparation [...exp]ectations for schools but also grounded licensure on [administra]tors' ability to demonstrate through their portfolio [...] to successfully perform as a school or district admin[istrator ...]

[...speci]alist approach to leadership provision include the [...innov]ation and the lower risk if individual programmes [... an] unregulated market are that certain offerings may [...lackin]g knowledgeable and skilled leaders. The ISLLC [...potenti]al for a measure of standardisation without the [...app]roach. However, significant criticisms of US

Education and Culture deems important for school administration' (p. 44).

In England, there is a tension between the emerging emphasis on personalised learning, for example in the redesign of the NPQH, and the need to adhere to National Standards for Headteachers to gain the state licence to practise as a school principal. The central question is 'what degree of individualisation is consistent with the award of a standardised national qualification?' This should form part of the evaluation of the new programme but an initial hypothesis is that personalisation will be more about the diversity of learning options available to candidates than about the formal assessment process leading to the award.

An important dimension of a personalised values-based approach to leadership development is the attention given to diversity issues. Lumby and Coleman (2007: 107) claim that 'the training programmes for all educational leaders both in the USA and England are unlikely to deal systematically with issues of diversity and social justice'. Bush et al. (2007) show that there was no differentiation for black and minority ethnic leaders within the NPQH and argue for an approach that recognises and celebrates their culture. As Lumby and Coleman (2007: 63) persuasively argue, 'the encouragement of diversity amongst leaders must mean that the training and development is not intended to re-create potential leaders from BME communities as clones of their white colleagues'. The implication here is that 'white' values are privileged over those of minority groups. Genuine personalisation requires an approach that respects and encourages ethnic diversity.

In South Africa, with its unique history, the language of management development is replete with discussion of desegregation and transformation. 'Achieving equitable access to education' is one of two key priorities outlined by the Task Team for Education Management Development (Department of Education 1996: 13). More recently, the ACE: School Leadership programme stresses the importance of 'the values of equity, access, transparency and democracy' (Department of Education 2007: 7). This language is aspirational but there is only limited evidence of equitable access to education more than a decade after the election of the country's first majority government. Most black African children are still educated in schools with poor facilities and under-trained teachers. This example illustrates the reality that values have to be translated into policies and practice if real change is to occur.

Towards a model for leadership development

The research and literature discussed in this book show that the need for training and development for heads and other school leaders is gaining wide, even global, acceptance (Watson 2003a). While there is great diversity in the extent and nature of provision, interest is growing and many countries are introducing or refining initiatives to produce a cadre of specialist leaders, who are appropriately prepared for their demanding roles. However, Huber (2003: 273) is right to claim that some nations have engaged with the issue more rigorously than others: 'While in some countries discussions of school leader development are mainly rhetoric, elsewhere concrete steps have been taken to provide significant development opportunities for school leaders.' Despite such differences, the intellectual case for training and support is overwhelming and the debate has now moved on to a consideration of the nature of such development. There are five main issues:

- Pre-service or in-service training?
- Centralised or pluralist programmes?
- Certification or ad hoc learning?
- School-based or on-campus provision?
- Who provides the training?

In addressing these themes, it is vital to recognise that 'solutions must be crafted to the local context' (Hallinger 2003b: 290).

Pre-service or in-service training?

The ideal model is to provide specific development opportunities *before* leaders, and in particular principals, take up their posts. The problems and challenges of leadership will not wait until in-service training has been completed. The confidence and competence of leaders needs developing ahead of their appointment to leadership posts. This will also satisfy selection panels that applicants are suitably qualified to fill their vacancies. Such pre-service preparation provides what Crow (2004) describes as 'professional socialisation', an introduction to the generic requirements of a particular leadership post such as principal. In Canada, England and the USA, for example, candidates seeking to become principals must have the requisite qualification.

However, this question should not be addressed as if these options are polar opposites. A more appropriate view is that leadership development should be ongoing, in tune with the contemporary interest in lifelong learning. Pre-service preparation needs to be followed by an effective induction programme, to facilitate organisational socialisation (Crow 2004). Subsequently, appropriate ongoing development opportunities should be made available to leaders so that they can update their knowledge and refine their leadership skills. The best example of continuing leadership development (CLD) is that provided by the NCSL, whose Leadership Development Framework (NCSL

2001) outlines five stages of provision from middle leaders to consultant headship. This approach is not appropriate everywhere but it is worthy of examination wherever leadership development is taken seriously and education budgets are sufficient to allow this 'ideal' model to apply.

In developing countries, however, funding is rarely sufficient to under preparation and training for all school leaders. In such circumstances, it sense to deploy the limited resources on principals. Bush and Oduro advocate focusing on in-service development because it targets fundin ple who are already holding the position rather than those who some point in the future. This stance is taken in Botswana, where may apply for training only after they have been in post for a years (Pheko 2008). The obvious problem with this mode is 'feel ill equipped for the post' (ibid.). In South Africa, a pr this issue has been taken. In inviting provinces to nom pilot ACE: School Leadership programme, both curren were eligible even though the course is ultimately programme for aspiring principals. The rationale tory stance is that current principals may feel heads of departments receive training, whic ment of Education 2007).

Such difficult decisions must be take is needed is a targeted donor progra countries. Given the British gover leadership of the current and pre for the English NCSL, it is surp ership development in this

Centralised or plur

Regardless of wh to consider wh pluralist ap involved predom of a Progr relations Education, t 2003). The out needs of Singapore measured by successive

programmes remain (for example, Bjork and Murphy 2005; Brundrett 2001). Only 15 per cent of universities providing preparation programmes are members of the University Council for Educational Administration (UCEA), suggesting that quality remains uneven.

Certification or ad hoc learning?

The growing international interest in leadership development has prompted some countries to introduce formal leadership qualifications. These are sometimes mandatory for those seeking appointments as principals. The merit of certification is that recruitment bodies may have a degree of confidence that the candidate has achieved at least threshold competence as an aspiring school leader. As noted earlier, this is too important to be left to chance.

France provides a clear example of the connection between training and selection. The Ministry of Education is solely responsible for the qualification process, which is administered by the Centre Condorcet in Paris. Qualification programmes are the responsibility of 28 academies throughout France, which must adhere to the prescribed legal guidelines. Following successful completion of this training, candidates are appointed as deputy school leaders for a two-year trial period, during which further training is required. Certification is closely integrated with the appointments process and successful candidates are guaranteed an appointment (Huber and Meuret 2004).

England will be moving closer to this approach in 2009 when the NPQH becomes mandatory for first-time heads. The 'new model' design shows that it should be seen as preparation for headship and not as a general professional development programme (www.ncsl.org.uk/npqh). As NPQH will provide the only route to headship, it can be seen as a state licensing process (Gunter, in press). The NCSL also provides the Early Headship Provision, incorporating 'New Visions'. Unlike the French model, this induction provision is not mandatory but the NCSL exhorts new heads to take the programme in strong terms; EHP 'is intended to be an official and formal recognition of the achievement of becoming a headteacher ... while participation is not compulsory, we believe New Visions gives headteachers the invaluable opportunity to reflect on their learning' (www.ncsl.org.uk/ehp). While this induction programme is not certificated, there is a clear intent to link the NPQH with selection and the subsequent induction programme.

As we noted earlier, new principals and assistant principals in Canada and most of the USA require a master's degree in educational administration before they can be considered for appointment. This requirement is well established but has become tighter since the introduction of the ISLLC (see above), described by Brundrett (2001: 234) as 'a centralising dictum'. The USA di from England and France by retaining a central role for universities. This is also evident in Singapore where the LEP is delivered by the National Institute of Education in partnership with the Ministry of Education (Chong et al. 2003). The Scottish Qualification for Headship (SQH) is also provided by universities, which must meet the requirements of the Standard for Headship in Scotland (SHS) (Reeves et al. 2001).

The South African ACE programme has been designed by a national body, the National Management and Leadership Committee (NMLC), which is led by the Department of Education and includes representatives of the 12 universities involved in delivering the pilot programme or expected to participate in subsequent phases of the programme. The evaluation findings will influence whether this is to become a mandatory national certificate for aspiring principals.

In most small island states, there are no such formal requirements, although potential principals in the Seychelles are expected to obtain the MA qualification offered in conjunction with the University of Warwick (Barallon, in preparation; Bush 2005). Bezzina (2002: 11) states that, in Malta, 'all prospective principals need to be in possession of a diploma in educational administration and management or its equivalent', a requirement introduced in 1994.

Despite their evident diversity, all these systems require candidates to acquire appropriate certification before practising as principals. This contrasts with those nations where there is a broad variety of development programmes available through a range of providers. Such arrangements exist in Denmark, the Netherlands and New Zealand, where 'it is not always easy for the potential participant to understand the quality of the programs that are available on the market' (Huber 2004c: 18). A more fundamental criticism is that certain countries are apparently content to allow their schools to be led and managed by people who may or may not be qualified, may or may not have undertaken any specialised preparation, and may or may not be suitable for the onerous responsibilities implicit in the principalship role. The continuing prevalence of such 'ad hoc' approaches suggests that many countries still underestimate the significance of leadership preparation for successful schooling. Certification is an essential component of any serious approach to leadership development, although this does not have to be 'nationalised' to be effective.

School-based or on-campus provision?

Traditional professional development programmes tend to be based on the campus of the host organisation, often a university department of education. Participants travel to the campus for set-piece lectures or seminars, and for individual tutorials with university staff. In most countries, attendance is part-time and candidates continue with their full-time professional role. This model has several advantages. First, it facilitates access to library facilities so that participants can access the research and literature, which are the staple diet of such programmes. Secondly, it provides opportunities for networking with peers. As we saw earlier, this is often regarded as the main benefit of leadership development activities (Bush et al. 2007b).

Many university-led programmes, including those in Canada, South Africa and the USA, incorporate field-based elements. However, they are often subordinate to the classroom aspects. An alternative approach is to regard the 'workplace as the workshop'. The NCSL (2007: 17) says that 'a large amount of learning should take place in school' rather than through courses. The emphasis is on developing 'craft' knowledge, 'knowing what works' (ibid.). While work-based learning can 'feel' authentic, it can also be narrow and conservative (ibid.: 18). The challenge is to find an appropriate balance of these elements that meets the needs of each client group. In South Africa, for example, the intention is that 50 per cent of ACE candidates' learning will be work-based, comprising activities planned, executed and evaluated at participants' schools (Department of Education 2007).

Who provides the training?

University-based courses are typically led and delivered by faculty, who may have good research records but often do not have school leadership and management experience. Many departments address this problem by also hiring staff with a background as principals, deputy principals or middle managers in schools. Academic life is often a second career for such professionals. In Canada and the US, for example, researchers work alongside former principals to deliver programmes for aspiring principals. The latter's 'craft' knowledge is allied to the academics' research expertise to produce a programme blending knowledge and understanding with practical school-based elements.

Bjork and Murphy (2005) report that US programmes have strengthened their 'field connections' since the 1980s, partly by hiring part-time 'adjunct' faculty who are often practising administrators. Similarly, the Principals' Qualification Program (PQP) in Ontario is usually delivered by staff and mentors who are experienced educational leaders (Huber and Leithwood 2004). While these 'veterans' often have a good understanding of the school context, the approach may be criticised for promoting a conservative approach to leadership development, based on current and previous practice rather than the future needs of schools and leaders (Crow 2004).

Designing, delivering and assessing leadership programmes are not straightforward tasks and require a complex skills set, including leadership expe-

understanding of relevant research and literature, and highly developed oral and written communication skills. Particularly where the field is expanding, countries may experience a lack of suitable course leaders and staff. Capacity-building should be seen as important for those who lead programmes as well as those who embark on them.

Bolam (2004) discusses the challenge facing academics in British university departments of education who are expected to produce high-quality research and publications to satisfy the demands of the Research Assessment Exercise (RAE). This activity is invariably regarded as more important than leading and delivering leadership development programmes. 'There are few, if any, incentives for staff to engage in such work in research-ambitious universities' (ibid.: 259). In the English context, the power and national reputation of the NCSL has contributed to a decline in university leadership programmes. The College's success owes a great deal to its skill in encouraging practitioner research, and in developing headteachers to become consultant leaders and contribute to programmes as facilitators, consultants and coaches (www.ncsl.org.uk/programmes).

Overview

The five questions addressed above provide a starting point for the construction of a model for school leadership development (see Table 9.1).

Table 9.1 'Nationalised' leadership development

Pre-service
Centralised
Certified
School-based
Practitioner-led

In the past decade, there has been a global trend towards more systematic provision of leadership and management development, particularly for school principals. Hallinger (2003a: 3) notes that, in 1980, 'no nation in the world had in place a clear system of national requirements, agreed upon frameworks of knowledge, and standards of preparation for school leaders'. In the twenty-first century, many countries are giving this a high priority, recognising its potential for school improvement.

This trend is encapsulated most powerfully by the English NCSL but it can ⊃ be seen in France, Singapore and South Africa. Candidates undertake 'cen- ⁓ed' training before becoming principals and receive national accreditation ⁓cessful completion of the activity. Much of the development work is work based, recognising that leadership practice takes place in schools. Current or former principals are involved in designing, leading and delivering leadership programmes, showing that 'craft' knowledge is increasingly respected.

This model does not apply everywhere but the trend is clear. Leadership preparation is no longer an optional activity, where professionals choose from an 'a la carte menu'. Rather, new principals require certification to practise, so that teachers, parents, school communities and governments can be satisfied that their schools will be led by qualified people. Even in the USA, where provision is pluralist, the advent of the ISLLC standards has created a measure of consistency across programmes. The case for systematic, specialised training for principals is persuasive and increasingly accepted. Leadership development has been 'nationalised'. It remains to be seen if this model produces more successful schools.

References

Achinstein,B. and Athanases, S., (2006) *Mentors in the Making: Developing New Leaders for New Teachers*. New York: Teachers College Press.

Afonso, N. (2003) 'The situation in Portugal', in L. Watson (ed.), *Selecting and Developing Heads of Schools: Twenty-Three European Perspectives*. Sheffield: European Forum on Educational Administration.

Agezo, C.K. and Christian, G. (2002) 'The impact of economic environment on primary school attendance: a case study of Elmina in the Central Region of Ghana', *Journal of Educational Management*, 4(1): 137–43.

AlertNet (2005) 'Niger: free food needed now as millions teeter on the brink of famine', 14 July. www.alertnet.org/thenews/newsdesk/IRIN

Alimo-Metcalfe, B. (1998) '360 degree feedback and leadership development', *International Journal of Selection and Assessment*, 6(1): 35–44.

Allix, N.M. (2000) 'Transformational leadership: democratic or despotic?', *Educational Management and Administration*, 28(1): 7–20.

Amezu-Kpeglo (1990) *Educational Administrator Preparation: Survey of Training Needs of Headmasters*. Accra: Institute for Educational Planning and Administration (IEPA), University of Cape Coast.

Avolio, B.J. (2005) *Leadership Development in Balance: Made/Born*. London: Lawrence Erlbaum Associates.

Babyegeya, E. (2000) 'Education reforms in Tanzania: from nationalisation to decentralisation of schools', *International Studies in Educational Administration*, 28(1): 2–10.

Barallon, L. (in preparation) *Leadership Development in the Seychelles*, Mahe.

Bassett, S. (2001) 'The use of phenomenology in management research: an exploration of the learners' experience of coach-mentoring in the workplace', paper presented at the Qualitative Evidence-Based Practice Conference, Coventry, May.

Beare, H., Caldwell, B. and Millikan, R. (1992) *Creating an Excellent School*. London: Routledge.

Becaj, J. (1994) 'Changing bureaucracy to democracy', *Educational Change and Development*, 15(1): 7–14.

Bennett, N., Crawford, M., Levačic, R., Glover, D. and Earley, P. (2000) 'The reality of school development planning in the effective primary school: technicist or guiding plan?', *School Leadership and Management*, 20 (3): 333–51.

Bennis, W. and Nanus, B. (1985) *Leaders*. New York: Harper and Row.

Berzina, Z. (2003) 'Reflections on school headship in Latvia', in L. Watson (ed.), *Selecting and Developing Heads of Schools: Twenty-Three European Perspectives*. Sheffield: European Forum on Educational Administration.

Bezzina, C. (2001) 'From administering to managing and leading: the case of Malta', in P. Pashiardis (ed.), *International Perspectives on Educational Leadership*. Hong Kong: University of Hong Kong.

Bezzina, C. (2002) 'The making of secondary school principals: some perspectives from the island of Malta', *International Studies in Educational Administration*, 30(2): 2–16.

Billot, J. (2003) *A Case Study of School Principals in Tonga*. Auckland: Commonwealth Council for Educational Administration and Management.

Bjork, L. and Murphy, J. (2005) *School Management Training Country Report: The United States of America*. HEAD Country Report. Oslo: BI Norwegian School of Management.

Blackmore, J. (2006) 'Deconstructing diversity discourses in the field of educational management and leadership', *Educational Management, Administration and Leadership*, 34(2): 181–99.

Blase, J. and Blase, J.R. (1998) *Handbook of Instructional Leadership: How Really Good Principals Promote Teaching and Learning*. London: Sage.

Bloom, G., Castagna, C., Moir, E. and Warren, B. (2005) *Blended Coaching: Skills and Strategies to Support Principal Development*. New York: Sage.

Bolam, R. (1999) 'Educational administration, leadership and management: towards a research agenda', in T. Bush, L. Bell, R. Bolam, R. Glatter and P. Ribbins (eds), *Educational Management: Redefining Theory, Policy and Practice*. London, Paul Chapman Publishing.

Bolam, R. (2004) 'Reflections on the NCSL from a historical perspective', *Educational Management, Administration and Leadership*, 32(3): 251–67.

Bolam, R., McMahon, A., Pocklington, K. and Weindling, D. (1995) 'Mentoring for new headteachers: recent British experience', *Journal of Educational Administration*, 33(5): 29–44.

Bolman, L.G. and Deal, T.E. (1997) *Reframing Organisations: Artistry, Choice and Leadership*. San Francisco, CA: Jossey-Bass.

Bottery, M. (1999) 'Education under the new modernisers: an agenda for centralisation, illiberalism and inequality?', *Cambridge Journal of Education*, 29(1): 103–20.

Bottery, M. (2001) 'Globalisation and the UK competition state: no room for transformational leadership in education?', *School Leadership and Management*, 21(2): 199–218.

Brew-Ward, M. (2002) 'Parental attitudes towards girls' education and its implications for community action: the case of selected communities in the Central Region of Ghana, unpublished MPhil thesis, University of Cape Coast.

Brundrett, M. (2000) 'The question of competence: the origins, strengths and inadequacies of a leadership training paradigm', *School Leadership and Management*, 20(3): 353–69.

Brundrett, M. (2001) 'The development of school leadership preparation programmes in England and the USA: a comparative analysis', *Educational Management and Administration*, 29(2): 229–45.

Brundrett, M., Fitzgerald, T. and Sommefeldt, D. (2006) 'The creation of national programmes of school leadership development in England and New Zealand: a comparative study', *International Studies in Educational Administration*, 34(1): 89–105.

Buckland, P. and Thurlow, M. (1996) *An Audit of EMD Needs and Resources in South Africa*. Pretoria: Department of Education.

Burgoyne, J., Hirsh, W. and Williams, S.T. (2004) *The Development of Management and Leadership Capability and its Contribution to Performance: The Evidence, the Prospects and the Research Need*. DfES Research Report 560. London: Department for Education and Skills.

Bush, T. (1986) *Theories of Educational Management*. London: Harper and Row.

Bush, T. (1995) *Theories of Educational Management*. 2nd edn. London: Paul Chapman Publishing.

Bush, T. (1998) 'The National Professional Qualification for Headship: the key to effective school leadership?', *School Leadership and Management*, 18(3): 321–34.

Bush, T. (1999) 'Crisis or crossroads? The discipline of educational management in the late 1990s', *Educational Management and Administration*, 27(3): 239–52.

Bush, T. (2001) 'School organisation and management: international perspectives', paper presented at the Federation of Private School Teachers of Greece Conference, Athens, May.

Bush, T. (2002) 'Authenticity – reliability, validity and triangulation', in M. Coleman and A. Brigg (eds), *Research Methods in Educational Leadership and Management*. London: Paul Chapman Publishing.

Bush, T. (2003) *Theories of Educational Leadership and Management*. 3rd edn. London: Sage.

Bush, T. (2004) Editorial. 'The National College for School Leadership: purpose, power and prospects', *Educational Management, Administration and Leadership*, 32(3): 243–9.

Bush, T. (2005) 'School leadership in the twenty-first century: Seychelles and international perspectives', keynote paper at the first School Leadership conference, Victoria, May.

Bush, T. (2006) 'The National College for School Leadership: a successful English innovation?', *Phi Delta Kappan*, 87(7): 508–11.

Bush, T. and Chew, J. (1999) 'Developing human capital: training and mentoring for principals', *Compare*, 29(1): 41–52.

Bush, T. and Coleman, M. (1995) 'Professional development for heads: the role of mentoring', *Journal of Educational Administration*, 33(5): 60–73.

Bush, T. and Glover, D. (2003) *School Leadership: Concepts and Evidence*. Nottingham: National College for School Leadership.

Bush, T. and Glover, D. (2004) *Leadership Development: Concepts and Beliefs*. Nottingham: National College for School Leadership.

Bush, T. and Glover, D. (2005) 'Leadership development for early headship: the New Visions experience', *School Leadership and Management*, 25(3): 217–39.

Bush, T. and Heystek, J. (2006) 'School leadership and management in South Africa: principals' perceptions', *International Studies in Educational Administration*, 34(3): 63–76.

Bush, T. and Jackson, D. (2002) 'Preparation for school leadership: international perspectives', *Educational Management and Administration*, 30(4): 417–29.

Bush, T. and Joubert, R. (2004) 'Education management development and governor training in Gauteng: an overview', paper presented at the EMASA Conference, Port Elizabeth, May.

Bush, T. and Middlewood, D. (2005) *Leading and Managing People in Education*. London: Sage.

Bush, T. and Moloi, K.C. (2007) 'Race, racism and discrimination in school leadership: evidence from England and South Africa', *International Studies in Educational Administration*, 35(1): 41–59.

Bush, T. and Oduro, G. (2006) 'New principals in Africa: preparation, induction and practice', *Journal of Educational Administration*, 44(4): 359–75.

Bush, T., Coleman, M. and Glover, D. (1993) *Managing Autonomous Schools: The Grant-Maintained Experience*. London: Paul Chapman Publishing.

Bush, T., Coleman, M. and Si, X. (1998) 'Managing secondary schools in China', *Compare*, 28(2): 183–96.

Bush, T., Middlewood, D., Morrison, M. and Scott, D. (2005) *How Teams Make a Difference: The Impact of Team Working*. Nottingham: NCSL.

Bush, T., Bisschoff, T., Glover, D., Heystek, J., Joubert, R. and Moloi, K.C. (2006a) *School Leadership, Management and Governance in South Africa: A Systematic Literature Review*. Johannesburg: Matthew Goniwe School of Leadership and Governance.

Bush, T., Briggs, A.R.J. and Middlewood, D. (2006b) 'The impact of school leadership development: evidence from the "New Visions" programme for early headship', *Journal of In-Service Education*, 32(2): 185–200.

Bush, T., Glover, D. and Sood, K. (2006c) 'Black and minority ethnic leaders in England: a portrait', *School Leadership and Management*, 26(3): 289–305.

Bush, T., Joubert, R. and Moloi, K.C. (2006d) *Matthew Goniwe School of Leadership and Governance: Mid-term Evaluation*. Johannesburg: MGSLG.

Bush, T., Allen, T., Glover, D., Middlewood, D. and Sood, K. (2007) *Diversity and the National Professional Qualification for Headship*, Nottingham: National College for School Leadership.

Bush, T., Duku, N., Kiggundu, E., Kola, S., Msila, V. and Moorosi, P. (2007a) *The Zenex ACE: School Leadership Research: First Interim Report*. Pretoria: Department of Education.

Bush, T., Glover, D. and Harris, A. (2007b) *Review of School Leadership Development*, Nottingham: NCSL.

Bush, T., Purvis, M.T. and Barallon, L. (in press) 'Leadership development in small island states', in J. Lumby, G. Crow and P. Pashiardis (eds), *International Handbook on the Preparation and Development of School Leaders*, New York: Routledge.

Caldwell, B. (1992) 'The principal as leader of the self-managing school in Australia', *Journal of Educational Administration*, 30(3): 6–19.

Caldwell, B. and Spinks, J. (1992) *Leading the Self-Managing School*. London: Falmer Press.

Campling, L. and Rosalie, M. (2006) 'Sustaining social development in a small island developing state? The case of Seychelles', *Sustainable Development*, 14: 115–25.

Cardno, C. and Howse, J. (2004) *A Study of the Secondary School Principals' Role, Workload and Management Development Needs in the Fiji Islands*. Auckland: Commonwealth Council for Educational Administration and Management.

Centre for Educational Research and Innovation (CERI) (2001) *New School Management Approaches*. Paris: OECD.

Chin, J. (2003) 'Reconceptualising administrative preparation of principals: epistemological issues and perspectives', in P. Hallinger (ed.), *Reshaping the Landscape of School Leadership Development: A Global Perspective*. Lisse: Swets and Zeitlinger.

Chirichello, M. (1999) 'Building capacity for change: transformational leadership for school principals', paper presented at ICSEI Conference, San Antonio, 3–6 January.

Chong, K.C., Stott, K. and Low, G.T. (2003) 'Developing Singapore school leaders for a learning nation', in P. Hallinger (ed.), *Reshaping the Landscape of School Leadership Development: A Global Perspective*. Lisse: Swets and Zeitlinger.

Coleman, A. (2005) 'Current state of school leadership: review of key findings from the 2004 survey', paper presented at the British Educational Leadership, Management and Administration Society annual conference, Milton Keynes, September.

Coleman, A. (2007) 'Leaders as researchers: supporting practitioner enquiry through the NCSL research associate programme', *Educational Management, Administration and Leadership*, 35(4): 479–97.

Coleman, M. (2002) *Women as Headteachers: Striking the Balance*. Stoke-on-Trent: Trentham Books.

Coleman, M., Qiang, H. and Li, Y. (1998) 'Women in educational management in China: experience in Shaanxi province', *Compare*, 28(2): 141–54.

Collarbone, P. (2001) *Leadership Programme for Serving Heads: A Review*. Nottingham: National College for School Leadership.

Commonwealth Secretariat (1996) *Managing and Motivating Teachers under Resource Constraints: Training Headteachers to Face the Challenges*. London: Commonwealth Secretariat.

Crossley, M. and Holmes, K. (1999) *Educational Development in the Small States of the Commonwealth: Retrospect and Prospect*. London: Commonwealth Secretariat.

Crow, G. (2001) *School Leader Preparation: A Short Review of the Knowledge Base*. NCSL Research Archive. www.ncsl.org.uk/Crow

Crow, G. (2004) 'The National College for School Leadership: a North American perspective on opportunities and challenges', *Educational Management, Administration and Leadership*, 32(3): 289–307.

Crow, G. (2006) 'Complexity and the beginning principal in the United States: perspectives on socialisation', *Journal of Educational Administration*, 44(4): 310–25.

Cuban, L. (1988) *The Managerial Imperative and the Practice of Leadership in Schools*. Albany, NY: State University of New York Press.

Daming, F. (2003) 'Principal training and development in the People's Republic of China: retrospect and prospect', in P. Hallinger (ed.), *Reshaping the Landscape of School Leadership Development: A Global Perspective*. Lisse: Swets and Zeitlinger.

Daresh, J. and Male, T. (2000) 'Crossing the boundary into leadership: experiences of newly appointed British headteachers and American principals', *Educational Management and Administration*, 28 (1): 89–101.

Davies, B. (1996) 'Re-engineering school leadership', *International Journal of Educational Management*, 10(2): 11–16.

Davis, B. (2001) 'The Australian principals centre: a model for the accreditation and professional development of the principalship', *International Studies in Educational Administration*, 29(2): 20–9.

Davis, B. (2003) 'Developing leaders for self-managing schools: the role of a principal centre in accreditation and professional learning', in P. Hallinger (ed.), *Reshaping the Landscape of School Leadership Development*. Lisse: Swets and Zeitlinger.

Day, C., Harris, A. and Hadfield M. (2001) 'Challenging the orthodoxy of effective school leadership', *International Journal of Leadership in Education*, 4(1): 39–56.

Day, D.V. (2001) 'Leadership development: a review in context', *Leadership Quarterly*, 11(4): 581–613.

Dellar, G. (1998) 'School climate, school improvement and site-based management', *Learning Environments Research*, 1(3): 353–67.

Department for Education and Skills (DfES) (2004) *School Leadership: End to End Review of School Leadership Policy and Delivery*. London: DfES.

Department for Education and Skills (2004a) *National Standards for Headteachers*, London: HMSO.

Department for International Development (DfID) (2006) *Millennium Development Goal 2: Achieve Universal Primary Education*. London: DfID. www.dfid.gov.uk/mdg/education

Department of Education (1996) *Changing Management to Manage Change in Education*. Pretoria: Department of Education.

Department of Education (2007) *ACE: School Leadership Pilot Programme*. Pretoria: Department of Education.

Derks, S. (2003) 'The selection and development of headteachers in the Netherlands', in L. Watson (ed.), *Selecting and Developing Heads of Schools: Twenty-Three European Perspectives*. Sheffield: European Forum on Educational Administration.

Derouet, J.L. (2000) 'School autonomy in a society with multi-faceted political references: the search for new ways of co-ordinating action', *Journal of Education Policy*, 15(1): 61–9.

Drake, P., Pair, C., Ross, K., Postlethwaite, T. and Ziogas, G. (1997) *Appraisal Study on the Cyprus Educational System*. Paris: International Institute for Educational Planning.

Dressler, B. (2001) 'Charter school leadership', *Education and Urban Society*, 33(2): 170–85.

Earley, P. and Weindling, D. (2006) 'Consultant leadership – a new role for head teachers?', *School Leadership and Management*, 26(1): 37–53.

Easterly, W. and Kraay, A. (2000) 'Small states, small problems? Income, growth and volatility in small states', *World Development*, 28(11): 2013–27.

Erculj, J. (2003) 'The selection and development of headteachers in the Republic of Slovenia', in L. Watson (ed.), *Selecting and Developing Heads of Schools: Twenty-Three European Perspectives*. Sheffield: European Forum on Educational Administration.

Fabunmi, M. and Adewale, J.G. (2002) 'A path-analytic model of schooli situations and secondary school students' academic performance in Oyo State, Nigeria', *Journal of Educational Management*, 4(1), 46–59.

Fenech, J. (1994) 'Managing schools in a centralised system: headteachers at work', *Educational Management and Administration*, 22(2): 131–40.

Foreman, K. (1998) 'Vision and mission', in D. Middlewood and J. Lumby (eds), *Strategic Management in Schools and Colleges*. London: Paul Chapman Publishing.

Fouquet, J.M. (2006) *School Management Training Country Report: France*. HEAD Country Report. Oslo: BI Norwegian School of Management.

Frost, D and Durrant, J. (2002) 'Teachers as leaders: exploring the impact of teacher-led development work', *School Leadership and Management*, 22(2): 143–61.

Fullan, M. (1992) *Successful School Improvement*. Buckingham: Open University Press.

Gayer, G. (2003) 'The selection process and continuing education of school principals in the city of Helsinki, Finland', in L. Watson (ed.), *Selecting and Developing Heads of Schools: Twenty-Three European Perspectives*. Sheffield: European Forum on Educational Administration.

Gaziel, H. (1998) 'School-based management as a factor in school effectiveness', *International Review of Education*, 44(4): 319–33.

Gergely, L. (2003) 'The selection and development of headteachers in Hungary', in L. Watson (ed.), *Selecting and Developing Heads of Schools: Twenty-Three European Perspectives*. Sheffield: European Forum on Educational Administration.

Girls' Education Unit (2002) 'National Vision for Girls' Education in Ghana and Framework for Action: Charting the Way Forward', Accra: Ministry of Education, Youth and Sports.

Glatter, R. (1979) 'Educational policy and management: one field or two?', *Educational Analysis*, 1(2): 15–24.

Glatter, R. (1991) 'Developing educational leaders: an international perspective', in P. Ribbins, R. Glatter, T. Simkins and L. Watson (eds), *Developing Educational Leaders*. Harlow: Longman.

Gold, A., Evans, J., Earley, P., Halpin, D. and Collarbone, P. (2003) 'Principled principals? Values-driven leadership: evidence from ten case studies of 'outstanding' school leaders', *Educational Management and Administration*, 31(2): 127–38.

Green, H. (2001) *Ten Questions for School Leaders*. Nottingham: National College for School Leadership.

Gronn, P. and Ribbins, P. (2003) 'The making of secondary school principals on selected small islands', *International Studies in Educational Administration*, 31(2): 76–94.

Gunter, H. (1997) *Rethinking Education: The Consequences of Jurassic Management*. London: Cassell.

Gunter, H. (in press) 'New Labour and school leadership 1997–2007', *British Journal of Educational Studies*.

Hallinger, P. (1992a) 'The evolving role of American principals: from managerial to instructional to transformational leaders', *Journal of Educational Administration*, 30(3): 35–48.

Hallinger, P. (1992b) 'School leadership development: evaluating a decade of reform', *Education and Urban Society*, 24(3): 300–16.

Hallinger, P. (2001) 'Leading educational change in East Asian schools', *International Studies in Educational Administration*, 29(2): 61–72.

Hallinger, P. (2003a) 'The emergence of school leadership development in an era of globalisation: 1980–2002', in P. Hallinger (ed.), *Reshaping the Landscape of School Leadership Development: A Global Perspective*. Lisse: Swets and Zeitlinger.

Hallinger, P. (2003b) 'School leadership preparation and development in global perspective: future challenges and opportunities', in P. Hallinger (ed.), *Reshaping the Landscape of School Leadership Development: A Global Perspective*. Lisse: Swets and Zeitlinger.

Hallinger, P. (2003c) *Reshaping the Landscape of School Leadership Development: A Global Perspective*. Lisse: Swets and Zeitlinger.

Hallinger, P. and Bridges, E. (2007) *Preparing Managers for Action: A Problem-based Approach*. Dordrecht: Springer.

Hallinger, P. and Heck, R. (1998) 'Exploring the principal's contribution to school effectiveness: 1980–1995', *School Effectiveness and School Improvement*, 9: 157–91.

Hansen, B. (2003) 'The selection and development of principals in Iceland', in L. Watson (ed.), *Selecting and Developing Heads of Schools: Twenty-Three European Perspectives*. Sheffield: European Forum on Educational Administration.

Harber, C. and Davies, L. (1997) *School Management and Effectiveness in Developing Countries*. London: Cassell.

Hardy, M. (in press) 'How to achieve consultant practitioner status: a discussion paper', *Radiography*.

Hargreaves, A. and Fink, D. (2006) *Sustainable Leadership*, San Francisco, CA: Jossey Bass.

Harris, A. (2003) *Building Leadership Capacity for School Improvement*. Milton Keynes: Open University Press.

Harris, A. (2004) 'Distributed leadership and school improvement: leading or misleading?', *Educational Management, Administration and Leadership*, 32(1): 11–24.

Harrison, J., Dymoke, S. and Pell, T. (2006) 'Mentoring beginning teachers in secondary schools: an analysis of practice', *Teaching and Teacher Education*, 22(8): 1055–67.

Hartley, J. and Hinksman, B. (2003) *Leadership Development; A Systematic Review of the Literature*. Coventry: NHS Leadership Centre.

Hawkey, K. (2006) 'Emotional intelligence and mentoring in pre-service teacher education: a literature review', *Mentoring and Tutoring*, 14(2): 137–47.

Heck, R. (2003) 'Examining the impact of professional preparation on beginning school administrators', in P. Hallinger (ed.), *Reshaping the Landscape of School Leadership Development: A Global Perspective*. Lisse: Swets and Zeitlinger.

Herbohm, K. (2004) 'Informal mentoring relationships and the career processes of public accountants', *The British Accounting Review*, 36(4): 369–93.

Herriot, A., Crossley, M., Juma, M., Waudo, J., Mwirotsi, M. and Kamau, A. (2002) 'The development and operation of headteacher support groups in Kenya: a mechanism to create pockets of excellence, improve the provision of quality education and target positive changes in the community', *International Journal of Educational Development*, 22: 509–26.

Hill, P. (2001) 'What principals need to know about teaching and learning', University of Melbourne, paper presented to the National College for School Leadership Think Tank, London.

Hobson, A. and Sharp, C. (2005) 'Head to head: a systematic review of the research evidence on mentoring new head teachers', *School Leadership and Management*, 25(1): 25–42.

Huber, S. (2003) 'School leader development: current trends from a global perspective', in P. Hallinger (ed.), *Reshaping the Landscape of School Leadership Development: A Global Perspective*. Lisse: Swets and Zeitlinger.

Huber, S. (2004a) 'Context of research', in S. Huber (ed.), *Preparing School Leaders for the 21st Century: An International Comparison of Development Programs in 15 Countries*. London: RoutledgeFalmer.

Huber, S. (2004b) 'Washington, New Jersey, California, USA: extensive qualification programs and a long history of school leader preparation', in S. Huber (ed.), *Preparing School Leaders for the 21st Century: An International Comparison of Development Programs in 15 Countries*. London: RoutledgeFalmer.

Huber, S. (2004c) *Preparing School Leaders for the 21st Century: An International Comparison of Development Programs in 15 Countries*. London: Routledge-Falmer.

Huber, S. and Cuttance, P. (2004) 'New South Wales, Australia: development of and for a "learning community"', in S. Huber (ed.), *Preparing School Leaders for the 21st Century: An International Comparison of Development Programs in 15 Countries*. London: RoutledgeFalmer.

Huber, S. and Gopinathan, S. (2004) 'Singapore: full-time preparation for challenging times', in S. Huber (ed.), *Preparing School Leaders for the 21st*

Century: An International Comparison of Development Programs in 15 Countries. London: RoutledgeFalmer.

Huber, S. and Imants, J. (2004) 'The Netherlands: diversity and choice', in S. Huber (ed.), *Preparing School Leaders for the 21st Century: An International Comparison of Development Programs in 15 Countries.* London: RoutledgeFalmer.

Huber, S. and Leithwood, K. (2004) 'Ontario, Canada: qualifying school leaders according to the standards of the profession', in S. Huber (ed.), *Preparing School Leaders for the 21st Century: An International Comparison of Development Programs in 15 Countries.* London: RoutledgeFalmer.

Huber, S. and Meuret, D. (2004) 'France: recruitment and extensive training in state responsibility', in S. Huber (ed.), *Preparing School Leaders for the 21st Century: An International Comparison of Development Programs in 15 Countries.* London: RoutledgeFalmer.

Huber, S. and Robertson, J. (2004) 'New Zealand: variety and competition', in S. Huber (ed.), *Preparing School Leaders for the 21st Century: An International Comparison of Development Programs in 15 Countries.* London: RoutledgeFalmer.

Huber, S. and Rosenbusch, H. (2004) 'Germany: courses at the state-run teacher training institutes', in S. Huber (ed.), *Preparing School Leaders for the 21st Century: An International Comparison of Development Programs in 15 Countries.* London: RoutledgeFalmer.

Huber, S. and Schratz, M. (2004) 'Austria: mandatory training according to state guidelines', in S. Huber (ed.), *Preparing School Leaders for the 21st Century: An International Comparison of Development Programs in 15 Countries.* London: RoutledgeFalmer.

Hughes, M., Carter, J. and Fidler, B. (1981) *Professional Development Provision for Senior Staff in Schools and Colleges.* Birmingham: University of Birmingham.

Inkoom, E.A. (2005) 'Impact of community support towards the education of girls in the Sissala East and West Districts, Upper West Region, Ghana', unpublished MPhil thesis, University of the Cape Coast.

Isok, H. and Lilleorg, L. (2003) 'The professional head of a school: the case of Estonia', in L. Watson (ed.), *Selecting and Developing Heads of Schools: Twenty-Three European Perspectives.* Sheffield: European Forum on Educational Administration.

James, C. and Whiting, D. (1998) 'The career prospects of deputy headteachers', *Educational Management and Administration,* 26(4): 353–62.

James, K. and Burgoyne, J. (2001) *Leadership Development: Best Practice Guide for Organisations.* London:, Council for Excellence in Management and Leadership.

Johansson, O. (2003) Leadership and compulsory schooling in Sweden: What's going on? in Watson, L. (Ed.) *Selecting and Developing Heads of Schools: Twent-*

Three European Perspectives, Sheffield: European Forum on Educational Administration.

Johnson, N. (1991) 'Developing educational leaders in Australia: guidelines for tertiary courses', in P. Ribbins, R. Glatter, T. Simkins and L. Watson (eds), *Developing Educational Leaders*. Harlow: Longman.

Kaparou, M. and Bush, T. (2007) 'Invisible barriers: the career progress of women secondary school principals in Greece', *Compare*, 37(2): 221–37.

Kavouri, P. and Ellis, D. (1998) 'Factors affecting school climate in Greek primary schools', *The Welsh Journal of Education*, 7(1): 95–109.

Keough, T. and Tobin, B. (2001) 'Postmodern leadership and the policy lexicon: from theory, proxy to practice', paper for the Pan-Canadian Education Research Agenda Symposium, Quebec, May.

Kitavi, M. and van der Westhuizen, P. (1997) 'Problems facing beginning principals in developing countries: a study of beginning principals in Kenya', *International Journal of Educational Development*, 17(3): 251–63.

Klus-Stanska, D. and Olek, H. (1998) 'Private education in Poland: breaking the mould', *International Review of Education*, 44(2–3): 235–49.

Kogoe, A. (1986) 'Perceived administrative needs of school executives in Togo', *Comparative Education*, 22(2): 149–58.

Kouzes, J. and Posner, B. (1996) *The Leadership Challenge*. San Francisco, CA: Jossey-Bass.

Lafond, A. and Helt, J.P (2003) 'The appointment and training of headteachers in France', in L. Watson (ed.), *Selecting and Developing Heads of Schools: Twenty-Three European Perspectives*. Sheffield: European Forum on Educational Administration.

Lam. J. (2003) 'Balancing stability and change: Implications for professional preparation and development of principals in Hong Kong', in P. Hallinger (ed.), *Reshaping the Landscape of School Leadership Development*. Lisse: Swets and Zeitlinger.

Lambert, L. (1995) 'New directions in the preparation of educational leaders', *Thrust for Educational Leadership*, 24(5): 6–10.

Lauglo, J. (1997) 'Assessing the present importance of different forms of decentralisation in education', in K. Watson, C. Modgil and S. Modgil (eds), *Power and Responsibility in Education*. London: Cassell.

Leask, M. and Terrell, I. (1997) *Development Planning and School Improvement for Middle Managers*. London: Kogan Page.

Lein, E. (2003) 'The selection and development of headteachers in Norway', in L. Watson (ed.), *Selecting and Developing Heads of Schools: Twenty-Three European Perspectives*. Sheffield: European Forum on Educational Administration.

Leithwood, K. (1994) 'Leadership for school restructuring', *Educational Administration Quarterly*, 30(4): 498–518.

Leithwood, K. and Levin, B. (2004) *Assessing School Leader and Leadership Programme Effects on Pupil Learning: Conceptual and Methodological Challenges.* London: Department for Education and Skills.

Leithwood, K., Steinbach, R. and Begley, P. (1992) 'The nature and contribution of socialisation experiences in becoming a principal in Canada', in G. Hall and F. Parkay (eds), *Becoming a Principal: The Challenges of Beginning Leadership.* New York: Allan and Bacon.

Leithwood, K., Jantzi, D. and Steinbach, R. (1999) *Changing Leadership for Changing Times.* Buckingham: Open University Press.

Leithwood, K., Day, C., Sammons, P., Harris, A. and Hopkins, D. (2006) *Seven Strong Claims about Successful School Leadership.* London: Department for Education and Skills.

Levačic, R. (1995) *Local Management of Schools: Analysis and Practice.* Buckingham: Open University Press.

Levine, A. (2005) *Educating School Leaders.* Washington, DC: Educating Schools Project.

Lim, L.H. (2005) *Leadership Mentoring in Education: The Singapore Practice.* Singapore: Marshall Cavendish.

Lin, M.D. (2003) 'Professional development for principals in Taiwan: the status quo and future needs', in P. Hallinger (ed.), *Reshaping the Landscape of School Leadership Development: A Global Perspective.* Lisse: Swets and Zeitlinger.

Lulat, Y. (1988) 'Education and national development: the continuing problem of misdiagnosis and irrelevant prescriptions', *International Journal of Educational Development*, 8(4): 315–28.

Lumby, J. and Coleman, M. (2007) *Leadership and Diversity: Challenging Theory and Practice in Education.* London: Sage.

Lumby, J., Walker, A., Bryant, M., Bush, T. and Bjork. L. (in press) 'Research on leadership preparation in a global context', in M. Young, G. Crow, J. Murphy and R. Ogawa (eds), *Handbook of Research on the Education of School Leaders.* University Council for Educational Administration.

Male, T. (2001) 'Is the National Professional Qualification for Headship making a difference?', *School Leadership and Management*, 21(4): 463–77.

Male, T. (2006) *Being an Effective Headteacher.* London: Paul Chapman Publishing.

March, J.G. (1978) 'American public school administration: a short analysis', *The School Review*, 86(2): 217–50.

Mathews, P. (2003) 'Academic mentoring: enhancing the use of scarce resources', *Educational Management Administration and Leadership*, 31(3): 313–34.

McFarlane, A, McMahon, A. and Bradburn, A. (2003) *E-learning for Leadersh Emerging Indicators of Effective Practice.* Nottingham: NCSL.

McGill, I. and Beaty, L. (1995) *Action Learning: A Practitioner's Guide*. London: Kogan Page.

McLennan, A. (2000) 'Education governance and management in South Africa', unpublished PhD thesis, University of Liverpool.

McLennan, A. and Thurlow, M. (2003) 'The context of education management in South Africa', in M. Thurlow, T. Bush and M. Coleman (eds), *Leadership and Strategic Management in South African Schools*. London: Commonwealth Secretariat.

Middlewood, D. (1995) 'All shapes and sizes', *Principal Matters*, 7(3): 22–3.

Miller, T.W. and Miller, J.M. (2001) 'Educational leadership in the new millennium: a vision for 2020', *International Journal of Leadership in Education*, 4(2): 181–9.

Moos, L. (2003) 'The Danish "Skoleinspector" (principal)', in L. Watson (ed.), *Selecting and Developing Heads of Schools: Twenty-Three European Perspectives*. Sheffield: European Forum on Educational Administration.

Morgan, G. (1997) *Images of Organization*. Newbury Park, CA: Sage.

Mulford, B. (2004) 'Organisational life cycles and the development of the National College for School Leadership: an antipodean view', *Educational Management, Administration and Leadership*, 32(3): 309–24.

Murphy, J. and Shipman, N. (2003) 'Developing standards for school leadership development: a process and rationale', in P. Hallinger (ed.), *Reshaping the Landscape of School Leadership Development: A Global Perspective*. Lisse: Swets and Zeitlinger.

Murray, M. (2003) 'The selection and development of principals in the Irish Republic', in L. Watson (ed.), *Selecting and Developing Heads of Schools: Twenty-Three European Perspectives*. Sheffield: European Forum on Educational Administration.

National College for School Leadership (NCSL) (2001) *Leadership Development Framework*. Nottingham: NCSL.

National College for School Leadership (NCSL) (2006b) *Corporate Plan 2006–2009*. Nottingham: NCSL.

National College for School Leadership (NCSL) (2006c) *Leadership Succession: An Overview*. Nottingham: NCSL. www.ncsl.org.uk/tomorrow'sleaderstoday

National College for School Leadership (NCSL) (2007) *What we Know about School Leadership*. Nottingham: NCSL. www.ncsl.org.uk

Naylor, P., Gkolia, C. and Brundrett, M. (2006) 'Leading from the middle: an initial study of impact', *Management in Education*, 20(1): 11–16.

Newland, C. (1995) 'Spanish American elementary education 1950–1992: bureaucracy, growth and decentralisation', *International Journal of Educational Development*, 15(2): 103–14.

ewman, J. and Clarke, J. (1994) 'Going about our business? The managerialism f public services', in J. Clarke, A. Cochrane and E. McLaughlin (eds),

Managing School Policy. London: Sage.

Nilsson, P. (2003) Teacher demand and supply in Africa, *Working Paper No. 12*, Education International, Brussels.

Ng, H.M. (2001) 'A model on continuous professional development of school leaders', *International Studies in Educational Administration*, 29(2): 73–87.

Oduro, G.K.T. (2003) 'Perspectives of Ghanaian headteachers on their role and professional development: the case of KEEA district primary school', unpublished PhD thesis, University of Cambridge.

Oduro, G.K.T. and MacBeath, J. (2003) 'Traditions and tensions in leadership: the Ghanaian experience', *Cambridge Journal of Education*, 33(3): 442–5.

Oplatka, I. (2004) 'The principalship in developing countries: context, characteristics and reality', *Comparative Education*, 40(3): 427–48.

Osei, J. (2003) 'Assessment of causes of dropout among basic education girls', *The Ghana Teachers' Journal*, 1(1): 33–51.

Owolabi, S.O. and Edzii, A.A. (2000) 'Teacher management and support systems in Ghana: the case of Cape Coast Municipality', *Journal of Educational Management*, 4(1), 1–14.

Pansiri, N. (in press) 'An assessment of the quality of instructional leadership for quality learning since the introduction of the primary school management development project in Botswana', *Educational Management, Administration and Leadership*.

Pashiardis, P. (2003) 'The selection, appointment and development of principals of schools in Cyprus', in L. Watson (ed.), *Selecting and Developing Heads of Schools: Twenty-Three European Perspectives*. Sheffield: European Forum on Educational Administration.

Pashiardis, P. and Ribbins, P. (2003) 'On Cyprus: the making of secondary school principals', *International Studies in Educational Administration*, 31(2): 13–34.

Peterson, K. and Kelley, C (2001) 'Transforming school leadership', *Leadership*, 30(3): 8–11.

Pheko, B. (2008) 'Secondary school leadership practice in Botswana: implications for effective training', *Educational Management, Administration and Leadership*, 36(1): 71–84.

Pocklington, K. and Weindling, D. (1996) 'Promoting reflection on headship through the mentoring mirror', *Educational Management and Administration*, 24(2): 175–91.

Proctor-Thomson, S.B. (2005) *Constellations or Stars? What Is Being Developed in Leadership Development?* Lancaster: Centre for Excellence in Leadership.

Reeves, D.B. (2004) *Assessing Educational Leaders*. Thousand Oaks, CA: Corwin Press.

Reeves, J., Casteel, V., Morris, B. and Barry, P. (2001) 'Testing a standard for headship: outcomes from the initial evaluation of the Scottish Qualification for Headship programme', *International Studies in Educational Administration*, 29(2): 38–49.

Republic of Botswana (1994) *The Revised National Policy on Education*. Gaborone: Government Printers.

Revell, P. (1997) 'Who said the TTA stands for totalitarianism?', *Times Educational Supplement: Management Update*, 6 June: 13–14.

Rigg, C. and Richards, C. (2005) *Action Learning, Leadership and Organisational Development in Public Services*. London: Routledge.

Rizvi, M. (2008) 'The role of school principals in enhancing teacher professionalism: lessons from Pakistan', *Educational Management, Administration and Leadership*, 36(1).

Roeder, W. and Schkutek, H. (2003) 'The selection, training and further education of headteachers in Germany', in L. Watson (ed.), *Selecting and Developing Heads of Schools: Twenty-Three European Perspectives*. Sheffield: European Forum on Educational Administration.

Sackney, L. and Mitchell, C. (2001) 'Postmodern expressions of educational leadership', in K. Leithwood and P. Hallinger (eds), *The Second International Handbook of Educational Leadership and Administration*. Dordrecht: Kluwer.

Sackney, L. and Walker, K. (2006) 'Canadian perspectives on beginning principals: their role in building capacity for learning communities', *Journal of Educational Administration*, 44(4): 341–58.

Sala, J. (2003) ' The management of schools and headship in Spain', in L. Watson (ed.), *Selecting and Developing Heads of Schools: Twenty-Three European Perspectives*. Sheffield: European Forum on Educational Administration.

Sapra, C. (1991) 'Towards 2000 and beyond: preparation of educational leaders in India', in P. Ribbins, R. Glatter, T. Simkins and L. Watson (eds), *Developing Educational Leaders*. Harlow: Longman.

Sapre, P. (2002) 'Realising the potential of educational management in India', *Educational Management and Administration*, 30(1): 101–8.

Savery, L., Soutar, G. and Dyson, J. (1992) 'Ideal decision-making styles indicated by deputy principals', *Journal of Educational Administration*, 30(2): 18–25.

School Management Task Force (1990) *Developing School Management: The Way Forward*. London: HMSO.

Scott, F. (2001) 'Developing human resources for effective school management in small Caribbean states', *International Journal of Educational Development*, 21: 245–56.

Scurati, C. (2003) 'The selection and development of headteachers in Italy', in L. Watson (ed.), *Selecting and Developing Heads of Schools: Twenty-Three European Perspectives*. Sheffield: European Forum on Educational Administration.

Sebakwane, S. (1997) 'The contradictions of scientific management as a mode of controlling teachers' work in black secondary schools: South Africa', *International Journal of Educational Development*, 17(4): 391–404.

Sergiovanni, T. (1984) 'Leadership and excellence in schooling', *Educational Leadership*, 41(5): 4–13.

Sergiovanni, T.J. (1991) *The Principalship: A Reflective Practice Perspective*. Needham Heights, MA: Allyn and Bacon.

Shakeshaft, C. (1989) *Women in Educational Administration*. Newbury Park, CA: Sage.

Simkins, T. (in press) 'Outcomes of school leadership development work: a study of three NCSL programmes', *Educational Management, Administration and Leadership*, 37.

Simkins, T., Garrett, V., Memon, M. and Ali, R.N. (1998) 'The role perceptions of government and non-government headteachers in Pakistan', *Educational Management and Administration*, 26(2): 131–46.

Simkins, T., Coldwell, M., Caillau, I., Finlayson , H. and Morgan. A. (2006) 'Coaching as an in school leadership development strategy: experiences from Leading from the Middle', *Journal of In-Service Education*, 32(3): 321–40.

Slavikova, L. and Karabec, S. (2003) 'School management preparation in the Czech republic', in L. Watson (ed.), *Selecting and Developing Heads of Schools: Twenty-Three European Perspectives*. Sheffield: European Forum on Educational Administration.

Smith, P.A.C. (2001) 'Action learning and reflective practice in project environments that are related to leadership development', *Management Learning*, 32(1): 31–48.

Southworth, G. (1995) 'Reflections on mentoring for new school leaders', *Journal of Educational Administration*, 33(5): 17–28.

Southworth, G. (2002) 'Instructional leadership in schools: reflections and empirical evidence', *School Leadership and Management*, 22(1): 73–92.

Southworth, G. (2004) 'A response from the National College for School Leadership', *Educational Management, Administration and Leadership*, 32(3): 339–54.

Stanev, S. and Mircheva, V. (2003) 'The school director in Bulgaria', in L. Watson (ed.), *Selecting and Developing Heads of Schools: Twenty-Three European Perspectives*. Sheffield: European Forum on Educational Administration.

Starratt, R.J. (2001) 'Democratic leadership theory in late modernity: an oxymoron or ironic possibility?', *International Journal of Leadership in Education*, 4(4): 333–52.

Stott, K. and Trafford, V. (2000) 'Introduction', in K. Stott and V. Trafford (eds), *Partnerships: Shaping the Future of Education*. London: Middlesex University Press.

Sundli, L. (in press) 'Mentoring – a new mantra for education?', *Teaching and Teacher Education*.

Svecova, J. (2000) 'Privatisation of education in the Czech Republic', *International Journal of Educational Development*, 20: 127–33.

Taylor, P. and Rowan, J. (2003) 'The selection and development of headteachers in England', in L. Watson (ed.), *Selecting and Developing Heads of Schools: Twenty-Three European Perspectives*. Sheffield: European Forum on Educational Administration.

Tekleselassie, A. (2002) 'The deprofessionalisation of school principalship: implications for reforming school leadership in Ethiopia', *International Studies in Educational Administration*, 30(3) 57–64.

Thody, A., Papanaoum, Z., Johansson, O. and Pashiardis, P. (2007) 'School principal preparation in Europe', *International Journal of Educational Development*, 21(1): 37–53.

Thomas, H. and Martin, J. (1996) *Managing Resources for School Improvement*. London: Routledge.

Thrupp, M. (2005) 'The National College for School Leadership: a critique', *Management in Education*, 19(2): 13–19.

Tomlinson, H. (2003) 'Supporting school leaders in an era of accountability: the National College for School Leadership in England', in P. Hallinger (ed.), *Reshaping the Landscape of School Leadership Development*. Lisse: Swets and Zeitlinger.

Tsukudu, P. and Taylor, P. (1995) 'Management development support for head teachers of secondary schools in South Africa', in D. Johnson (ed.), *Educational Management and Policy: Research, Theory and Practice in South Africa*. Bristol: University of Bristol.

Tuohy, D. and Coghlan, D. (1997) 'Development in schools: a systems approach based on organisational levels', *Educational Management and Administration*, 25(1): 65–77.

Tusting, K. and Barton, D. (2006) *Models of Adult Learning: A Literature Review, NRDC Literature Review*. London: National Institute for Continuing Adult Education.

Underhill, C.M. (2006) 'The effectiveness of mentoring programs in corporate settings: a meta-analytical review of the literature', *Journal of Vocational Behaviour*, 68(2): 292–307.

Van der Westhuizen, P. and van Vuuren, H. (2007) 'Professionalising principalship in South Africa', *South African Journal of Education*, 27(3): 431–45.

Van der Westhuizen, P., Mosoge, M. and van Vuuren, H. (2004) 'Capacity-building for educational managers in South Africa: a case study of the Mpumalanga province', *International Journal of Educational Development*, 24: 705–19.

Varri, K. and Alava, J. (2005) *School Management Training Country Report: Finland*. HEAD Country Report. Oslo: BI Norwegian School of Management.

Waite, D. (2002) 'The "paradigm wars" in educational administration: an attempt at transcendence', *International Studies in Educational Administration*, 30(1): 66–81.

Wales, C. and Welle-Strand, A. (2005) *School Management Training Country Report: Norway*. HEAD Country Report. Oslo: BI Norwegian School of Management.

Walker, A. and Dimmock, C. (2004) 'The international role of the NCSL: tourist, colporteur, or confrere?', *Educational Management, Administration and Leadership*, 32(3): 269–87.

Walker, A. and Qian, H. (2006) 'Beginning principals: balancing at the top of the greasy pole', *Journal of Educational Administration*, 44(4): 297–309.

Walker, K. and Carr-Stewart, S. (2006) 'Beginning principals: experiences and images of success', *International Studies in Educational Administration*, 34(3): 17–36.

Wasserberg, M. (2000) 'Creating the vision and making it happen', in H. Tomlinson, H. Gunter and P. Smith. (eds), *Living Headship*. London: Paul Chapman Publishing.

Watson, K. (2001) 'Comparative educational research: the need for reconceptualisation and fresh insights', in K. Watson (ed.), *Doing Comparative Research: Issues and Problems*. Oxford: Symposium Books.

Watson, L. (2003a) 'Issues in the headship of schools', in L. Watson (ed.), *Selecting and Developing Heads of Schools: Twenty-Three European Perspectives*. Sheffield: European Forum on Educational Administration.

Watson, L. (2003b) *Selecting and Developing Heads of Schools: Twenty-Three European Perspectives*. Sheffield: European Forum on Educational Administration.

Weindling, D. (2004) *Funding for Research on School Leadership*. Nottingham: NCSL.

West-Burnham, J. (1997) 'Leadership for learning: reengineering "mind sets"', *School Leadership and Management*, 17(2): 231–43.

West-Burnham, J. (1998) 'Identifying and diagnosing needs', in J. West-Burnham and F. O'Sullivan (eds), *Leadership and Professional Development in Schools*. London: Financial Times–Prentice Hall.

West-Burnham, J. (2001) 'Interpersonal leadership', *NCSL Leading Edge Seminar*, Nottingham: National College for School Leadership.

Wolf, S. and Gearheart, M (1997) 'Issues in portfolio assessment: assessing writing processes from their products', *Educational Assessment*, 4(4): 265–96.

World Bank (2002) *Education and HIV/AIDS: A Window of Hope*. Executive Summary. Washington, DC: World Bank.

Young, M. (2006) 'Sharing leadership within and beyond the senior management team – case studies of three very large primary schools' unpublished PhD thesis, University of Lincoln.

Yukl, G.A. (2002) *Leadership in Organizations*. 5th edn. Upper Saddle River, NJ: Prentice-Hall.

Zagoumennov, Y. and Shalkovich, L. (2003) 'The selection and professional development of school directors in Belarus', in L. Watson (ed.), *Selecting and Developing Heads of Schools: Twenty-Three European Perspectives*. Sheffield: European Forum on Educational Administration.

Author index

Subject index